I0164424

Face Off with
an Ex-Priest

Karl Keating

RASSELAS
HOUSE

Copyright © 2017 Karl Keating

All rights reserved. No part of this work may be reproduced, stored in a retrieval system, or transmitted in any form or by any means without the prior written permission of the copyright holder.

Published by Rasselas House
El Cajon, California
RasselasHouse.com

Cover design by EbookLaunch.com
Formatting by PolgarusStudio.com

ISBN 978-1-942596-19-6 Paperback
ISBN 978-1-942596-18-9 Ebook

Contents

Contents

Introduction

My opponent in this debate was Bartholomew F. ("Bart") Brewer, a former Discalced Carmelite priest and, at the time we squared off, the head of Mission to Catholics International. The topic for the evening was "Is the Roman Catholic Church Christian?" His answer would be a firm "No." The venue was Calvary Baptist Church in National City, the town immediately to the south of San Diego. Calvary Baptist had the reputation of being the most ardently anti-Catholic church in the county, perhaps because Brewer's organization was headquartered on the church's property. His pastor served as moderator at the debate.

The crowd was not evenly-split. Of the 350 spectators, no more than 50 were Catholics. The remainder were Fundamentalists, and they seemed to come in two flavors: those predisposed, naturally enough, to favor my opponent, and those who already were zealous members of his (quite vocal) fan club.

There would have been more Catholics in attendance, no doubt, if the diocesan paper had advertised the debate in its upcoming events column, the way the main secular daily did, and if more parishes had published notices in their Sunday bulletins. All had press releases in ample time. But there long had been, in official Catholic circles, almost a denial that Fundamentalism was wooing Catholics away from the church of their upbringing, and even clerics who admitted such a problem existed tended to prefer a policy of benign neglect or were skittish about anything deemed controversial—and what's more controversial than a controversy?

The lack of publicity by Catholics may not have made much difference, since the venue surely scared off partisans of Rome. A priest I knew planned to attend but got cold feet—all the more understandable for Catholic laymen, few of whom might feel comfortable entering what they perceive to be hostile territory. From my point of view, though, it was more important to have an abundance of Fundamentalists in the audience. It was their minds that I hoped to change. Besides, I wasn't sure Brewer would debate anywhere except on his home ground. You take what you can get.

Another wrinkle: Brewer preferred not to have a true debate format, with multiple back-and-forths. We originally agreed to speak for 30 minutes each and then take questions, the whole show to be done in two hours. A couple of weeks before the debate he called and said he preferred to have us talk for 45 minutes each. A bit long, I replied, but all right. Did I have a preference in speaking order? he asked. Not really, I said, my suspicions not being aroused. Good, said Brewer. He wanted to go second, and so it was agreed. The debate would begin at 7:30 p.m., and we could still get people out by 10:00 p.m., allowing an hour for questions.

After an introduction by the pastor-moderator, I gave my remarks, emphasizing some of Fundamentalism's weak points, encouraging the audience to exercise skepticism when listening to anti-Catholics, and citing a few egregious bloopers by those who made their living attacking the Church. The audience was politely attentive, chuckling at the throwaway lines, leaning forward as I made my main points. It seemed some of my ideas were getting through. In retrospect, I can't say whether most listeners were thinking about what I was saying or just marveling that a Catholic had no fangs. Few of the Fundamentalists had ever heard a Catholic speak before. I had a sense of being on display. After the debate, many people came up to me, thanking me just for showing up, something they half-expected me not to do, I guess. After all, when they walked in, they probably thought "What could a Catholic possibly have to say?" They found out soon enough.

I hadn't timed my talk well. I took 50 minutes instead of the agreed-upon 45, yet the moderator hadn't admonished me. I felt both sheepish and grateful. My talk done, I sat in the front row, where Brewer had been waiting.

He ascended the pulpit, piled half a dozen books on one side and his Bible on the other. Adjusting the microphone, he started to preach. It took me a few minutes to understand what he was doing since I had expected a different kind of presentation. I should have known better.

Brewer started out louder than my loudest and then turned up the volume. In a few moments someone behind me called out, "Amen, brother!" He was echoed by others. Soon there were two or three dozen voices crying out. Brewer began more deliberately to play to the crowd. As though giving a political speech, he would make a pointed remark and then pause, giving his backers time to throw in some "amens" and an occasional "hallelujah."

I had heard him speak in a Baptist church before—that was before he knew me by sight, so he didn't know a Catholic was present—and I had seen him on a television talk show, listened to him on radio, and read his writings. Often enough I had been annoyed at his sharp phrasing but accepted it as his shtick, yet I admit to being surprised at the level of invective this night. He was on a roll. And he kept on rolling. 45 minutes, 50 minutes, an hour. He said he would talk on several main points, and he had at least one to go when, an hour-and-a-half into his presentation, he was interrupted by Catholics who had had enough. The moderator, who seemed to have forgotten that he was wearing a watch, got up and pulled Brewer from the pulpit.

I insisted on a few minutes' rebuttal. A little steamed (though not because of the logorrhea, which worked to my benefit by giving me the crowd's sympathy), I commented on Brewer's more bizarre charges, the worst of which—made while he was discoursing on the supposed non-existence of the priesthood—was that Pope Pius IX (reigned 1846–1878) "had three girlfriends" while pope. It was a canard, I remarked, noting that one could read about such slanders against Pio Nono in *No Popery*, written by Fr. Herbert Thurston, S.J., in 1930. This citing of a specific reference work seemed to take care of that issue, and I felt lucky to have stumbled across the book some months earlier. (You never know when obscure sources will come in handy.)

Then came questions. The moderator whispered to me that maybe the question period should be kept to a few minutes so people could get home, but I insisted questions be taken until no one had anything more to ask—a rash move on my part, since I ended up staying until 2:30 a.m. The crowd didn't have to stay quite that long; the formal question period ended around 11:30 p.m. (most people, bless 'em, were still present). About two-thirds of the questions were directed to me.

Many former Catholics came up to me and said they wish someone had told them about the Church while they were still in it. A Catholic whom I hadn't seen for years confided that she had been tempted to "unpope" but that the debate broke the spell. Several Fundamentalists said they were surprised that any case at all could be made for the Catholic religion; they seemed inclined to do some research on their own. One woman, who identified herself as a member of Calvary Baptist Church, said, "I'm not going to fellowship here any longer"—but that was less a reflection on my talk, I think, than on what she perceived as a setup.

Bart Brewer had been raised in Philadelphia. As a young man he thought he had a vocation to the priesthood, and he ended up being ordained for the Discalced Carmelite order. After a while his superiors sent him to the Philippines. The assignment did not last long, Brewer admitting in a tract that he got into some trouble there. Back in the U.S., he underwent a change of religious allegiance. First he became a Seventh-day Adventist because his mother had become one. Later he became a Baptist. At some indeterminate point he concluded that his calling was to undermine the Church he once had been part of. Perhaps it simply was that he wasn't trained for anything other than religious work and didn't see any other avenue open to him. He founded Mission to Catholics International and headed the organization for many years. ("International" was a bit misleading, since Brewer's touring and speaking seemed to be confined to the U.S.)

Although Brewer had received standard seminary training, he seemed to know little about Catholicism, other than that now he opposed it. In opposing it he adopted the tones of anti-Catholic Protestants of the nineteenth and earlier centuries, warning his listeners about dark "Papist" conspiracies as he showed them hosts (presumably unconsecrated) in a ciborium. He affected a Southern drawl, in emulation perhaps of television preachers he admired. It was as though such an accent were expected of one in his position, even someone who had grown up in the City of Brotherly Love. Along with the drawl came an unctuousness that brought to my mind Dickens' Uriah Heep.

Despite all that, I had a soft spot for Brewer, frustrating though I found him. Yes, he was an apostate priest who spoke cavalierly and inaccurately about his former faith, but he seemed to me a self-broken man. I couldn't help thinking that, deep down, he was disappointed with the hand he had been dealt—or that he had dealt to himself. This turned out to be the only debate he ever had with a Catholic, though he and I occasionally spoke about a rematch.

Notes on the Text

The following transcript has been edited for clarity and concision. I have taken the liberty of correcting grammatical errors and obvious misstatements, and I have removed those seemingly unavoidable hesitations and starts (ah's and um's and their cousins) that may not be particularly off-putting when spoken but seem to gouge the eyes when in print. The four debates in the series have been made roughly uniform in length. When given publicly, they ranged from two hours to an almost unendurable four hours, counting question-and-answer sessions. Each is now short enough to be read at a single sitting.

I have attempted to retain each speaker's best arguments, feeling no temptation to omit my opponents' most persuasive comments. (I think the Catholic position, however inadequately expressed by me, is match enough for any charge leveled against it.) I have omitted or truncated exchanges that were redundant or seemed unhelpful to the audiences. Also omitted have been audience questions that strayed too far from the topics of the debates or that were not true questions but attempted preaching sessions.

Looking back at my own arguments, particularly those made when on defense, I find places where I could have made a better reply. I have not gussied up my remarks. A reader may say, "But you could have said *this*!" My excuse must be that *this* didn't occur to me at that moment. Perhaps I was taken off guard. Perhaps my mind went blank. Perhaps I just didn't yet know the best answer and could offer only the second-best answer. What is presented here is verisimilitude. I can use a phrase from nineteenth-century German historian Leopold von Ranke. I have attempted to give the story "*wie es eigentlich gewesen*"—"how it really was."

And how it really is today. There is not a single anti-Catholic claim in these books that has fallen out of circulation. The claims have been around for lifetimes, and there is no likelihood that they ever will disappear completely, human nature and human obstinacy being what they are. I have tried to respond to the claims with candor and fairness. Whether I have succeeded is for readers to judge. Throughout the debates I kept in mind that "the truth shall set you free." I always have found searching for truth—and debating what is true—to be exhilarating. I hope you will too, as you read what follows, and I hope these pages bring solace and confidence to Catholics and intrigue and light to non-Catholics.

Debate Transcript
Karl Keating vs. Bartholomew F. Brewer

MODERATOR: A couple of people have asked me, is there going to be a fight? We don't plan on having one. Seriously though, this is something that we have worked on for several months, myself and Bart Brewer and Karl Keating. We met together several months ago and determined the date to have this meeting. And we, I think, consider each other our friends, and we are here for a legitimate debate and, through mutual consent, Mr. Keating is going to be our first speaker. And he will be given 45 minutes for his time. When he is finished, Mr. Brewer will come, and he will have 45 minutes. Then we will have a question-and-answer time.

KEATING: First, my thanks to Bart Brewer for agreeing to this public discussion. Then to our host for so kindly agreeing to let us use the church and for taking on the responsibility of moderator. He tells me that I might well be the first Catholic to speak from this pulpit. Depending on how things go, I might very well be the last. Apparently, some people hope so.

A few days ago, my office received an anonymous phone call. The man said that tonight's debate is the work of the Devil. It's actually quite the opposite. The one thing the Father of Lies doesn't want is for people to come together in a friendly discussion to search for the truth because he fears we might find it. If that caller isn't pleased that I'm here, perhaps it might please him to find that I'm at a considerable disadvantage tonight. After all, it's easier to attack the Catholic religion than to defend it. An attack can be phrased in just a few words. A defense might take paragraphs or pages. Normally an attack has three elements. One is that there is something completely true in it. Second, there's something true but so abruptly stated that it's misleading and so its implication is incorrect. The third element is simply false. The Catholic apologist must try to untangle the web in far too short a time.

Mr. Brewer and I have not compared notes. We don't know what each other will be speaking about tonight. I don't know the specific charges he'll make, but in the last few years I've read his materials, and I know that he's made dozens. Obviously, I'm unable to anticipate them all. If, after his talk, I could keep you here until this time tomorrow, I could answer every objection he brings up, but my lungs and your posteriors won't last that long. Maybe we can touch on a few of the points in the question session.

My goal tonight isn't to prove to you the truth of the Catholic religion. There isn't time for that. I'd be satisfied to suggest to you that what you've heard about the Catholic religion from anti-Catholics you ought to take not just with a grain of salt but with the whole salt shaker. You haven't been told the whole story.

To Catholics who are in the audience I say, "Have confidence in your religion." In the last few years I've been asked hundreds of questions regarding the Catholic religion. I by no means have had all the answers on the tip of my tongue. As you'll see, I won't have them on the tip of my tongue tonight. But when I say to an inquirer, "Let me look it up and I'll get back to you tomorrow," in each case I've been able to find an answer that satisfies not just me as a believing Catholic but also the person who put the question to me. He may not agree with the answer, but at least he sees what the Catholic position is.

To Fundamentalists I say, "Reserve judgment until you have a chance to see what knowledgeable Catholics say about their religion. Be cautious in swallowing charges that might be unflattering. Do some homework on your own. Stop and wonder why, if even a portion of the charges you've heard are true, the Catholic Church, and the Catholic religion, didn't collapse in a paroxysm of laughter centuries ago."

Let me take a look at things from the view point of the common Catholic.

If you're a Catholic you certainly have been through it. It's the middle of the afternoon on a Saturday, and there is a knock at the door. You open it to find a man with a wide smile, a Bible in his hand, and a question on his lips. "Have you been saved, friend?" You tell him that you're a Catholic, in hopes that it will scare him away, which it does not. He leans over and takes out of his valise several Catholic versions of the Bible. "Which do you think we should use?" he says, "New American Bible, Jerusalem Bible, maybe the old Douay-Rheims?" You engage him in conversation for a while, and you end up merely frustrated. He goes away with an air of triumph, and you go away with a sore throat.

Or the altercation—somehow it always seems to end up being an altercation—might happen after Mass. You exit church to find people passing out tracts excoriating the Eucharist. If you so much as look one of them in the eye, he comes toward you. The crowd of Mass-goers is so large that you can't wiggle your way through fast enough. You can't escape. When the man reaches you, he says, "Here, read this. It will tell you about the idolatry of the Mass." "No thanks," you say, "not interested." So he proceeds to tell you, word for word, just what you would have read. As he does that, he backs you toward the curb. You listen to him or you step into whizzing traffic.

Or, it might happen in a social setting, say, after your pro-life group has concluded its business meeting. Everybody sits back for a little conviviality and a spot of tea, and a born-again sidles up to you and says, "Wouldn't you like an assurance of salvation?" You begin to answer by saying, "Yes, but . . ." She waves you to be quiet, and she flips through a heavily underlined New Testament to look for the objection to the comment you never got a chance to make. From there it is all downhill.

These discussions, whether with the man at the door, or the people outside of church, or the woman at the social setting, seem to go nowhere. You know things are being taken out of context but you can't remember what the context is. There are snappy rejoinders coming to mind, but they never quite manifest themselves. Later, you kick yourself for not having said the right thing. If you put Catholic beliefs into your own unconsidered words, you find out all you've done is put your feet in your mouth. You've confirmed your adversary's worst suspicions, and the worst thing is that for some questions you don't have the vaguest hint of an answer. You begin to think that, God forbid, the Fundamentalist might be on to something.

On the other hand, if you're a Fundamentalist, you have a different perspective. You may have been brought up in Fundamentalism. Maybe you're a convert from some other religion, maybe even from Catholicism. Regardless, your view of the Catholic religion is largely negative. It strikes you as a strange amalgamation of some things that are true and, mostly, things that are untrue. You have the impression that it's at once Western and Eastern, that it has something to do with the capitals of the West, such as Paris and London, and something to do with the exotic capitals of the East, such as Baghdad, Cairo, and New York.

The Catholics you meet are pretty much like other people. Some are smart; some are not. You've heard that there are more than a billion of them in the world, and you suspect they can't all be stupid, but sometimes you wonder what it is they see in their religion. You don't worry about it particularly because you've been told that their priests and their bishops hoodwink them and that the people swallow everything they hear from the pulpit. You've been told a lot of other things about the Catholic religion. Some are true, many are not, but you don't know which are which. You accept them all because you don't know why you shouldn't.

You have been told, for example, that the Catholic religion didn't start until the reign of the Emperor Constantine, in the early fourth century. Or maybe that it didn't start until the reign of Pope Gregory the Great at the turn of the seventh century. Now that happens to be historical nonsense, but you've never looked it up in a history book to see for yourself. You just accept it as being true. You've heard that Catholics pay to get their sins forgiven in confession. You never have come up to a Catholic and asked if that's so. If you did, he'd laugh at you the same way you'd laugh at him if he said, "Is it true that in Fundamentalist services you just sit around all morning thumping Bibles?" You've heard that between New Testament times and the Reformation there were lots of churches that weren't connected with Rome, that opposed what many people called the Roman system, that were basically the same as today's Fundamentalism, but you've never been told names and dates for the very good reason that there were no such groups.

I want to take representative examples of these charges or impressions and look at them at some length. Let's begin with a historical question: was Peter ever in Rome? It's not a major point. The world doesn't turn on it, but you always find anti-Catholics bringing it up. I think it's probably best stated by Loraine Boettner in his book *Roman Catholicism*. Boettner, as many of you know, was the dean of American anti-Catholics. Every major anti-Catholic organization, and probably all the minor ones, relied heavily on his work. He says, "The remarkable thing about Peter's alleged bishopric in Rome is that the New Testament has not one word to say about it. The word 'Rome' occurs only nine times in the Bible and never is Peter mentioned in connection with it. There is no allusion to Rome in either of his epistles. Paul's journey to the city is recorded in great detail. There is, in fact, no New Testament evidence, nor any historical proof of any kind, that Peter was ever in Rome. All rests on legend."

Well, what about it? Admittedly, the scriptural evidence for Peter being in Rome is thin. Nowhere does the Bible say unequivocally that he was there. On the other hand, it doesn't say he wasn't. But Boettner is wrong when he says that there is no allusion to Rome in Peter's epistles. There is, in the greeting at the end of the first epistle where he says, "The Church, here in Babylon, united with you by God's election, sends you her greeting, and so does my son Mark." "Babylon" was a code word for Rome. It's used that way five times in the Book of Revelation. In extra-biblical works such as the Sibylline Oracles and the Apocalypse of Baruch and the Fourth Book of Esdras, which were all written about the same time, it's again used that way, quite clearly, to mean Rome. Boettner says, "But there is no good reason for saying that Babylon means Rome. Why didn't he [Peter] just say Rome?" Well, the good reason is called "persecution."

Peter was known to the authorities as a leader of the Christian Church, and the Church, under Roman law, was organized atheism. The worship of any gods other than the Roman was considered atheism. Peter would do himself no favor, nor would he do a favor to those connected with him, by advertising his presence in the capital, which he might very well have done by sending letters out saying, "Here I am in Rome." Peter was a wanted man. All Christians were, so he had a good reason to hide his location.

In any event, let's be generous. Let's say that an opponent of Catholicism, in good faith, can say that Peter wasn't in Rome, if he looks only at the Bible. But he shouldn't put on historical blinders. He should look at historical works of roughly the same period to see what they say. Clement of Rome, who later would be the fourth pope, or the third successor to Peter, wrote his letter to the Corinthians and made reference to Peter ending his life where Paul ended his. We all know Paul died at Rome. Ignatius of Antioch, in the year 110, in his letter to the Romans remarked that he wasn't in a position to command the Romans the way Peter and Paul had been. This indicates that Peter, like Paul, had been in Rome. Irenaeus, writing later in the second century, said that Matthew wrote his Gospel while Peter and Paul were evangelizing in Rome and laying the foundation of the Church there.

There are other ancient writings that could be cited, and they all speak to the same. There is no ancient writing that claims that Peter ended up in a city other than Rome and died there. No other city ever laid claim to him. Boettner, like many other Fundamentalist apologists, said "exhaustive research by archaeologists has been made, down through the centuries, to find some inscription in the catacombs and other ruins of ancient places that would indicate Peter, at least, visited Rome. But the only things found to give any promise were a few uncertain bones."

Boettner saw his book through the presses in 1962. Some years later Pope Paul VI was able to issue a report on the archeological excavations that took place under the high altar in Peter's Basilica, excavations that began after World War II. They demonstrated conclusively that Peter's bones and his grave were there. For example, most of the graves next to where his grave was located say something like "Peter is here." They can be dated to the first century.

I've discussed Peter's presence in Rome at some length, but I don't want you to think this is the only historical point on which Boettner and other anti-

Catholics are in error. It's fair to say that in Boettner's book of 460 pages there is, on average, one major blunder per page. The most obvious weaknesses of the anti-Catholic position relate to history. This is where the faults of anti-Catholic pundits are most glaring. Many charges against the Church rely on imaginary and sometimes falsified history. Take away that history and the charges collapse. I will not resist giving you a few juicy examples.

Some Fundamentalists argue against papal infallibility, which was defined formally at the First Vatican Council in 1870, by quoting a speech supposedly given by Bishop Joseph Strossmayer of Croatia. The gist of the supposed speech is that Strossmayer just finished reading the New Testament through and now he comes before the Fathers of the Council and says, "Gentlemen, I've read the New Testament, and there is no evidence of a papacy in its pages." Well, the problem is that the speech attributed to Strossmayer is a well-known forgery. You can check the *Catholic Encyclopedia*, which will tell you that. If you don't like the *Catholic Encyclopedia*, go to the books it cites, some by non-Catholics. Every Protestant scholar who's written a book about Vatican I will have the same story. They all, Catholic and Protestant, agree the speech is phony.

I correspond with a Fundamentalist, a young fellow who used to be a Catholic. He said, finally, after we went back and forth on this, "Okay, I admit the Strossmayer speech a forgery, but I'm going to keep distributing the speech anyway because its theology is true." Well, what can you say about that attitude?

When it comes to Transubstantiation, which is the technical name for turning bread and wine into the body and blood of Christ during the Mass, Fundamentalists say, "That didn't come into being until the year 1215 at the Fourth Lateran Council." But all you have to do is pick up Ignatius of Antioch, writing in 110. He condemned people who did not confess that the Eucharist is the flesh of our Savior, Jesus Christ. So you can't very well say that 1,105 years later the doctrine was made up. Similarly, Boettner said it wasn't until the eleventh century that the Mass was declared a sacrifice, but in the second century Irenaeus wrote a book where he specifically said that it was.

Many anti-Catholics say confession to a priest didn't arise until the Middle Ages, but in the third century Origen wrote that for absolution a distinct accusation or admission of the sins—a listing of them—would be required, and confession had to be made privately to a priest.

In many matters anti-Catholic commentators leave listeners with the wrong notion of what happened. It said that in 1572 Pope Gregory XIII was so pleased that the Huguenots—that is, French Protestants—were massacred on Bartholomew's Day that he ordered hymns of praise to be sung and a medal to be struck in celebration. These commentators don't tell you the real facts. They don't tell you that the Queen Mother of France, Catherine de' Medici, was the real power behind the throne of her weakling son, Charles IX. She organized the plot against the Huguenots. The problem, in her mind, was that the king's chief minister happened to be a Protestant. She didn't want him to have influence over her son, so what better way to get rid of him than to claim that there was an uprising by Protestants? He and many others were done away with.

Fundamentalists commentators who bring up the story also don't tell you that Catherine arranged to have the French ambassador go to the papal court and tell the pope, "Your Holiness, it was a coup attempt. The Protestants tried to kill the king." The pope had no reason to doubt the report and therefore had hymns of praise sung, and he had a medal struck. But when he found out the truth, he roundly condemned the king and the king's mother.

You've heard people talk against relics. The most common argument is that, if you take all the relics of the True Cross and you put them together you've got enough wood to build a ship. What anti-Catholics don't tell you, because they probably don't know, is that in the nineteenth century a Frenchman named Charles Rohault de Fleury cataloged and measured all known relics of the True Cross. He computed that their total volume wouldn't make up more than one-third of a cross. So, there is a scandal concerning the Cross, but the scandal isn't that there are so many pieces floating around that you could build a ship. The scandal is: what happened to the rest of the True Cross?

Some Fundamentalists—and I'm thinking here for example of the author of a book called *The Mystery of Babylon Revealed*—say that under the Inquisition as many as 95 million people were killed in Europe. Keep in mind that the Inquisition didn't operate throughout Europe. It was restricted to southern France, Spain, Italy, and the southern part of Germany. It never was in England, never in Scandinavia, and never in Eastern Europe. The present-day population of the areas where it operated doesn't approach 95 million. The population was only a fraction of that when the Inquisition existed. Scholars, both Catholic and Protestant, say that number of deaths is exaggerated between 10,000 and 50,000 times. The figure of 95 million isn't a typographical error. It's an example of bad faith in writing against a Church that one opposes.

Consider Ralph Woodrow. Some of you have read his book *Babylon Mystery Religion*, which is not to be confused with *The Mystery of Babylon Revealed*. Woodrow's thesis is that Catholicism arose out of Babylonian sun worship. He tries to prove this by using photographs of the interior of St. Peter's Basilica in Rome. You've all seen pictures of that interior. You've seen Bernini's twisted columns and the great baldachin over the high altar. On one such photo Woodrow superimposes an arrow pointing to the back wall, at what appears to be a sunburst. He says, "See, that sunburst proves that Catholics worship the sun." Unfortunately for Woodrow, he didn't have a clear photograph of the interior of St. Peter's. If he had, he would have seen that what his arrow pointed at was not a representation of the sun but a representation of the Holy Spirit in the form of a dove exuding rays of light.

Frank Sheed was well known as a Catholic street corner preacher, an author, and a publisher. He said that you can't stop people from drawing true inferences from true facts. If the fact is that Jesus rose from the dead, certain things follow. You don't stop there, even if that would be all that the Bible said on the incident. If Jesus said "This is my body" at the Last Supper, certain things follow from that. You can't prevent people from trying to find out rationally what those things might be. This is doctrinal development, drawing true conclusions from true facts. Fundamentalists have their own brand of doctrinal development. They too believe things that are not found on the face of Scripture—for example, the Trinity. The word "Trinity" cannot be found in the Bible. Its first use is by Theophilus of Antioch in 181. A Fundamentalist will say, "The word may not be in the Bible, but the doctrine is there." That's what Catholics say when Fundamentalists say, "Hey, the word 'Transubstantiation' is not in the Bible." That's true. It's a term of art just as "Trinity" is a term of art. But the doctrine is there.

There are other things that Fundamentalists say don't find warrant in Scripture. Some of them believe that drinking, dancing, and gambling are immoral without exception, yet you won't find in the Bible across-the-board condemnations of those activities. You'll find only condemnations of their abuse. When it comes to wine, some Fundamentalists go so far as to say that Christ didn't drink any. That's hard to believe when in his first miracle he turned jugs of water into wine. The host of the wedding had plenty of wine, he thought, but the guests consumed it all. Jesus made, miraculously, a large amount of additional wine. In a sense he was inviting the people to drink further, an indication that he approved of drinking wine.

Consider next salvation and justification. For Catholics, salvation depends on the state of the soul at death. Christ has already redeemed us; he's unlocked the gates of heaven, so to speak. He did his part, and now we have to cooperate. He will not save us without our cooperation. You won't get to heaven unless you follow his instructions. If we're to pass through the gates into heaven, we have to be spiritually alive. If a soul is in a purely natural state, suffering from the penalties of original sin, it's without sanctifying grace and is spiritually dead.

For Fundamentalists sanctifying grace is just a figment of Catholics' imagination. What matters is accepting Christ as your Lord and Savior. When you do that, Christ covers your sinfulness. He turns a blind eye to it. It's as though he hides your soul under a cloak. Any soul hidden under the cloak is admitted to heaven, no matter how putrescent the soul beneath the cloak. No one without the cloak, no matter how pristine, will be admitted to heaven.

The Reformers saw justification as a legal act by which God declares the sinner to be meriting heaven, even though his soul remains objectively sinful and unjust. It's not a real eradication of sin but a covering or non-imputation. It's not a real renewal or a real sanctification, only an external application of

Christ's justice. The soul doesn't actually become holy.

The Catholic Church understands it differently. Justification is a true eradication of sin, a true sanctification of the inner man. The soul becomes objectively pleasing to God, objectively good, and so it merits heaven. It merits heaven because it is good now. Scripture conceives of forgiveness of sins as a complete removal of them. In the Psalms the terms used are "blot out" and "clears away." Isaiah also uses "blots out." John says "takes away." When the Bible mentions "covering," in almost all those cases it refers not to God forgiving sins but to us ignoring one another's sins.

On the positive side, the Bible shows that justification is a re-birth. In John and Titus we learn that it's a generation of a supernatural life in a former sinner. It involves, as Paul says in Ephesians, an inner renewal and, in First Corinthians, a real sanctification. The soul itself becomes beautiful and holy. It's not an ugly soul hidden under a cloak. Because it's beautiful and holy, it can be admitted to heaven where, the Bible says, "nothing unclean shall enter." An ugly soul hidden under a cloak is still unclean and does not get admitted to heaven.

Now an allied topic, the assurance of salvation. There are verses in the Bible that call this notion into doubt. "I buffet my own body and make it my slave, for I, who have preached to others, may myself be rejected," says Paul in I Corinthians. He also says, "Beloved, you have always shown yourselves obedient, and now that I am at a distance, you must work to earn your salvation in anxious fear." Some translations say "in fear and trembling." That's not the language of self-confident assurance. Paul also tells us, "All of us have a scrutiny to undergo before Christ's judgment seat, for each to reap what his mortal life has earned, good or ill according to his deeds. God will award to every man what his acts have deserved." But if the only act of consequence is being saved, a one-time event, what difference do all the other acts make, as far as your salvation goes?

These verses demonstrate that we'll be judged by what we do, not just by the one act of whether we accept Jesus as our Savior. But it's not to be thought that being a do-gooder is sufficient. The Bible is quite clear that we're saved by faith. The Reformers were right to say that. To that extent they merely repeated ancient doctrine. Where they erred was in saying that we are saved by faith alone. Luther admitted, when he translated the Bible into German, that he foisted in the word "alone." It is not there in the Greek. He admitted that. He also admitted that he wanted to get rid of the Epistle of James and throw it out of the Bible. He called it "an epistle of straw" because it specifically says that we are not saved by faith alone. But Luther didn't have the gumption to do that.

Consider Romans 5:2: "We are confident in the hope of attaining glory as the sons of God." The saints in heaven do not have the virtue of hope. They don't have the virtue of faith. They don't need faith because they see God. They don't need hope because they've already achieved what they hoped for on Earth. They have only the third theological virtue, charity. But Paul says that we, Christians on Earth, have hope. "Our salvation is founded on the hope of something. Hope would not be hope at all if its object were in view." That doesn't mesh with the notion of an assurance of salvation. "Are you saved?" inquires the Fundamentalist. "I'm redeemed," says the Catholic, "and, like the apostle Paul, I'm working out my salvation in fear and trembling, with hopeful confidence but not with a false assurance. And I do this as the Church has taught through all the centuries."

The Reformers rejected the papacy and they rejected, therefore, the teaching authority of the Church. They looked elsewhere for it and they thought they found the rule of faith in the Bible. They really didn't have anywhere else to look. But reason and experience tell us the Bible can't be each man's private guide to the truth. If individual guidance were a reality, we'd see every Christian believing the same thing. It does no good to say that we believe the same on the major points. You would have to believe the minor points identically also because, if the Holy Spirit enlightens you, he's not going to distinguish between major and minor points. He would enlighten you completely. He would not teach you error.

It has to be acknowledged that the Bible nowhere says it's the sole rule of faith. It never phrases it that way. It even denies it. At the end of John's Gospel the evangelist says that not everything concerning Christ's life is recorded in the Gospels. Presumably, that includes some of his teachings. Paul says in

Second Timothy, "Much Christian teaching is to be found in the tradition which is handed down, by word of mouth." In Second Thessalonians he says, "Stand fast and hold the traditions which you have learned, whether by word or by our epistle."

The early Christians knew the fullness of the faith was handed down orally. They were the people who, as Acts puts it, "occupy themselves continually with the apostles' teaching." That was long before any of the New Testament was written. Fundamentalists make noises about Christ condemning traditions. "Why is it that you, yourselves, violate the commandments of God with your traditions?" he says to the Pharisees. Paul warned, "Take care not to let anyone cheat you with philosophizing, with empty fantasies drawn from human tradition." But these, obviously, refer to erroneous human traditions, mainly those that were handed down by the Jews and were supplementary to the original Mosaic Law.

Let me just say something addressed more to Catholics than to Fundamentalists. Whatever forces might drive a man to Fundamentalism—and it has to be granted that emotional factors play a part—he remains a Fundamentalist for doctrinal reasons. He might have left his previous church, whatever it was, because he didn't like the priest or minister or because people in the congregation were rude to him, but that's not why he sticks with Fundamentalism. Those emotional pushes and pulls are short-lived. He could have found a minister as eloquent, or congregants as friendly, at the mainline Protestant church down the street. No, the reason he stays in the Fundamentalist church is doctrine. His conversion had to do with doctrine. Many Catholics think Fundamentalism isn't so much a matter of theology but of pathology. They think Fundamentalists lack roots, they're at odds with their culture, they feel lost and lonely—that's why they're Fundamentalists.

One well-known Catholic scholar, Fr. Eugene LaVerdiere, wrote a tract called "Fundamentalism a Pastoral Concern." He said that the only genuinely Christian response to Fundamentalism is the life and work of Jesus. He said the answer is not a biblical argument but the strength of faith and the power of love. Putting it crudely, he said the only way to conquer Fundamentalism is to love it to death. Although it's true that people switch religions partly for emotional reasons, Catholics who once were Fundamentalists and have come back to the Church deny that loneliness and the like were the things that kept them Fundamentalists. Whatever emotional reasons they may have had for leaving the Church of Rome, they decided its teachings were untrue.

People who come back to the Catholic Church from Fundamentalism come back for the same reason. They come back for doctrinal reasons. They admire the truth that is in Fundamentalism—and there is much truth there—but they see that Fundamentalism is only a partial truth and that the fullness of truth can only be found in Rome. The committed Fundamentalist is convinced the Catholic Church is wrong, and he thinks he can prove it from the Bible. Glad-handing isn't going to suffice to get him a better picture of the Church. He's not going to change his mind just by smiling at him. He wants Catholics to explain the Bible and points of history. Unless Catholics do that, he won't be satisfied, and he shouldn't be satisfied. It's been on the level of doctrine that Fundamentalism has achieved its considerable power in this country. This power lies not in the objective truth of the Fundamentalist position, since Fundamentalism is a mixture of truth and error, but in the fact that Fundamentalists say God's truth matters and that we must act upon it, whatever its consequences. Who says A, must say B. That's the attraction, and it's a powerful attraction.

If Catholics expect to answer the Fundamentalist challenge to the Church, they are going to have to answer not just with the heart but also with the head. After all, it's the truth that sets us free. I think, at least on that point, we can all agree. Thanks for your kind attention.

MODERATOR: Just as Mr. Keating is the founder and leader of Catholic Answers, Mr. Brewer is the founder and leader of Mission to Catholics. It's interesting that both groups have the same status as far as the government is concerned. They are both incorporated as non-profit corporations, and I'm sure the speakers can attest to that—no profit. Mr. Brewer is a former Catholic priest, now an ordained Baptist minister. He'll come now and make his presentation.

BREWER: I want to thank the moderator for allowing my friend Karl Keating and me to use this beautiful auditorium. I want to thank you people for being here. I know many of my preacher friends are here tonight, from all over. And many of my relatives are here. I want to thank you lovely people for coming here tonight. I know you've come from near and far. That's very gracious. And, please, remember as I offer my presentation tonight, indeed my aim is to speak the truth in love.

My presentation tonight is not a scientific, historical, or philosophical defense of biblical Christianity but instead a declaration of God's Word, for his Word is above his name. Truth is not something you dialogue. Truth is not something you debate. Truth is something you declare. Truth is something you proclaim. And so tonight, beloved, please pay close attention to biblical content which will expose as false, as non-Christian, four major areas of Roman Catholic teaching: the Roman Catholic priesthood; the Roman Catholic sacrifice for the Mass, which would include Transubstantiation; the Roman Catholic concept of biblical authority; and the Roman Catholic concept of soteriology or salvation.

As a youngster growing up in Philadelphia, my home parish was the cathedral of Sts. Peter and Paul, where the rector, Hubert Cartwright, later Bishop Cartwright, often said that the Brewer family was more Roman Catholic than Rome. There was the daily Mass, weekly confession, the daily recitation of the rosary in the utmost respect, I mean the utmost respect for every Catholic priest, every Catholic nun. There was a God consciousness. I mean there was a Christ reverence, beloved. We were serious about God. We were serious about the Church of Rome. I know I wanted God's holy will in my life. I wanted to please God. I sincerely thought that God was calling me to be a Roman Catholic priest, so I chose the Discalced Carmelite order, perhaps one of the more strict, one of the more ancient of the religious orders in the Church of Rome.

Never did I question, nor did anyone else, my vocation, my calling to the Catholic priesthood, during those twelve years of formal religious, academic training or formation. Nor did I entertain, for a moment, any contrary teaching, any practice, because for us, for me, the voice of the Church was the voice of God. We made no formal distinction between the two.

On ordination day I heard the all seminarian choir sing, "Thou art a priest forever, according to the order of Melchizedek." When I heard that sung, at the Shrine of the Immaculate Conception of Mary in Washington, D.C., I was ecstatic with joy. Through the invocation of the Holy Spirit, and the laying on of hands, according to the gospel of Rome, when the bishop invoked the Holy Spirit and placed his hands upon my head, I was ordained to the priesthood of Jesus Christ. According to Romanism, I was ordained a priest forever. But, thank God, it was not to be forever. "When the veil of the temple was rent in twain from the top to the bottom" (Mark 15:38). That did away with the Old Testament priesthood. The letter to the Hebrews which, by the way, the Church of Rome is not too excited about, makes it very clear that the sacerdotal, sacrificial system of the Jews is consummated and superseded in Jesus Christ, the risen Savior.

There is no organized, special, sacrificing, mediating, hierarchical priesthood this side of Calvary. And by the way, we're not dealing with biblical interpretation tonight, really. I would hope and pray that we're dealing with the plain facts of God's word, the Bible.

Hebrews 7 makes it clear that the priesthood of Jesus Christ belongs to him and no one else. It may not be shared in. Please remember that. His priesthood is unchangeable. His priesthood is untransmissible. His priesthood is non-transferable. There is no priesthood today except the priesthood of all believers, according to Peter and John. There is one God and one mediator between God and men, the man Christ Jesus, who gave himself a ransom for all.

The theory of a mediating, sacrificing, official priesthood mainly started with an individual by the name of Cyprian. Cyprian was a great theological authority, in the West, until the time of Augustine and later was endorsed by Roman Catholicism. You find nothing in the New Testament about a sacrificing, mediating priesthood. Absolutely nothing, either explicitly or implicitly, in the pure wheat of God's word, the Bible.

Less than 300 years after our Savior's ascension, there were all kinds of heresies. In fact, as you know, Paul told the Corinthians that heresies were necessary because they would distinguish the true believer from the make-believer. Augustine said that between the first century and the fifth century there were something like 80 heresies. In fact, only 100 years after Pentecost, much of the truth had already become so concealed that its real meaning was almost lost. One does not have to be a Church historian to see how the soil for Roman Catholicism was prepared long before that church came into existence. It was a beginning of that apostasy which furnished the soil for the Church of Rome. The Roman Catholic system is the logical result.

Had there been no Roman Catholic system, necessity would have dictated that something fill the void left by the apostasy that Paul spoke about, that Paul predicted. Romanism is simply a perversion of true Christianity. Romanism cannot claim to be the Church of the New Testament. The Roman Catholic Church, with her popes, bishops, priests, and ritual actually claims to excel, claims to excel, mind you, the Church of the New Testament.

Beloved, I believe that smacks of arrogance and pride. The Roman Catholic priesthood has no root or foundation whatsoever in God's word, in the Bible. Frequently people ask, "Bart, what does a priest do? What is he doing all day? What is his work like? What kind of routine does he follow?" His day begins with Mass. Every morning he goes to the altar and there "renews the sacrifice by which Christ wrought our redemption." The Church of Rome teaches that Christ offered the first Holy Mass. Mass is said to be identical with Calvary; it is a continuation of Calvary. In fact, Romanism, the papal system, teaches that the Mass is not a mere re-dramatization or a mere re-enactment of Calvary. Oh no, the Church of Rome teaches that it is one and the same, that it is identical with Calvary.

As a Romish, papal priest, because of my great ignorance of the Word of God, I offered or celebrated or said over 4,000 Masses during my ten years as a Roman Catholic priest. I was taught that Jesus Christ, offering the sacrifice of the Cross, offers a Holy Mass as our High Priest, and the invisible head of the Church, using the priests of his Church as instruments. That's what I was taught. I knew that Golgotha was unique. I knew that. I knew it happened once in history. I knew it was enough to atone for the sins of man, but, mark you, I was also told that in the Mass, in the sacrifice of the Mass, both for the living and for the dead, this atonement is supplied to the souls of men, women, and children. In other words, through the Roman Catholic Mass, the body and blood of Jesus Christ are constantly being mystically sacrificed and presented to the Father in heaven. It is an everlasting extension of a redemption. There is no end. That's why there are four Masses beginning every second of the day, in some part of the world.

One of the oldest, most superficial arguments, perpetrated by Rome, is from Malachi 1:11: "For from the rising of the sun even unto the going down of the same, my name shall be great among the Gentiles, and in every place incense shall be offered unto my name in a pure offering. My name shall be great among the heathen, said the Lord of Hosts." Romanism says that "the sacrifice of the Cross cannot be meant, as this was offered at one place only. Prophecy is fulfilled in the Holy Sacrifice of the Mass, which is offered in all parts of the world."

But wait a minute, beloved, listen; we are not to be naïve. We're not to be simplistic, are we? You mean to tell me we are to succumb to a lot of pious religious rhetoric? The Bible tells us not to twist the word of God, and I charge the Church of Rome tonight for butchering what is plain and clear and explicit in God's word, the Bible. Now if you will, Peter warned about those who will twist the writings of Paul. And even the apostle Paul warned the Corinthians about those who will corrupt or change or chop or butcher or vandalize or twist the Holy Word of God, the Bible. And so we are to be scrupulous, beloved. We're not to be ignorant. We are told to study the word of God, amen? And then we are to rightly divide the word of truth. We are to cut it straight. You and I have that serious responsibility, do we not? I say that because a close look at the meaning of this text, and I'm referring to Malachi 1:11, indicates not a literal, external offering but a spiritual, internal offering.

By the way, it's very interesting, when a Roman Catholic apologist refers to the Church Fathers, he will not tell you that there are three categories of Church Fathers: genuine, dubious, and spurious. That's why when we go to the so-called Church Fathers, we better do our homework, because it's conceivable that one may quote a spurious or dubious Church Father.

You know, folks, to a great extent the so-called Church Fathers in the post-apostolic era were biblically, theologically unsound. May I say that again? I hope it doesn't sound like heresy. I believe many of the Church Fathers were biblically, theologically unsound. Yet, in many ways, they were clearly opposed to the Church of Rome. I mean to what later on became Roman Catholic teaching and practice. Let me give you an example from John Chrysostom. Okay, this is what he said in reference to the Christian sacrifice. He said, "And through him we offer a sacrifice to God." What sacrifice does he mean? He himself has explained, saying, "The fruit of the lips which confess his name: prayers, hymns, thanksgiving. These are the fruit of the lips. They offered sheep and calves, given to the priest, but we offer none of these things but thanksgiving and the imitation of Christ in all things as far as it is possible. May our lips thus blossom forth. Be not forgetful while doing a liberality, for with such sacrifices God is well pleased. Let us give to him such a sacrifice that he may offer it to the Father." And here's another statement by John Chrysostom, who lived in the fourth century: "But who taketh away the sins of the world? As if he were always doing it. For he did not only take then when he suffered, but from that time to the present he takes away sins. He is not always crucified, for he offered one sacrifice for sins, but he always purifies by that one sacrifice."

Recently, a Roman Catholic professor back East tried to show me from the Old Testament, from the Bible, that there is a root or a foundation for the Roman Catholic sacrifice of the Mass. Where do you think he went? You have any notion? Genesis 14:18, where it says that Melchizedek brought bread and wine because he was a priest of the Most High God. In this context, Melchizedek offered no sacrifice because the author of the letter to the Hebrews, describing the character and conduct of Melchizedek, says nothing of sacrifice. Now, beloved, if it's there, love me enough to show me. But it simply is not there, in the Bible, not your Catholic Bible, not my translation. If Melchizedek did offer bread and wine, he did so as a type of Christ's offering on the Cross, for Melchizedek was a type of Christ. I had no power to consecrate, or convert, or transubstantiate elements like bread and wine into the literal body and blood, soul and divinity, bone and marrow, of the

Lord Jesus Christ. That is nothing more than sorcery. That's what it is. That is sorcery.

Show me, from God's word, the Bible. There is no word about it, yet, on ordination day, the bishop said, "Receive thou power to offer sacrifice and to celebrate Masses, both for the living and for the dead." What heresy. That hurts the heart of God. Folks, that kind of teaching stinks. That kind of teaching has no support whatsoever in God's word, the Bible. I'll tell you why. The Bible tells us why: because the apostles were commanded to preach the Gospel, not to offer sacrifice. The theory of a sacrificing priesthood with an earthly sanctuary is absolutely contrary to Holy Scripture.

As early as the last part of the second century, or maybe the third century, the heathens were calling the early Christians—and by the way they were not Roman Catholic—the heathens were calling the early Christians atheists because they had no altar, no priesthood, no sacrifice. That's right. Athanagoras, in response to those who were antagonistic to the early Christians, declared, "Those who charge us with atheism have not the faintest conception of what God is. Foolish and utterly unacquainted with natural and divine things, they measure piety by the rule of sacrifices. As to our not sacrificing, the Framer and Father of this universe does not need blood nor the odor of burnt offerings nor the fragrance, needing nothing, either within or without. The noblest sacrifice is to know who stretched out the heavens, who adorned the sky with stars and made the earth to bring forth seed of every kind, who made animals and fashioned man. We lift up holy hands to him. What need has he further of the Hecatomb? Yet, it does behoove us to offer a bloodless sacrifice and the sacrifice of our reason."

And then the great [Anglican] Bishop [Joseph] Lightfoot has gone through the Christian writings of the second century and shown how far they are from the sacerdotal priesthood of Roman Catholicism. I notice my friend, Mr. Keating, mentioned Clement of Rome, but again, beloved, we've got to be scrupulous with historical facts. As I said before, there are three categories of Church Fathers according to Roman Catholic authorities. You had the genuine Church Fathers, and then you had the dubious, and then you had the spurious. In the epistles of Clement of Rome, Polycarp, and Barnabas and in the *Shepherd of Hermes*, even in the epistles of Ignatius, there is no trace of a priesthood with daily sacrifice. Justin Martyr admits that Christianity had its priests and sacrifices, but the priests are the Christian people, and the sacrifices are spiritual.

Isn't that something? Does that grab you, or not? Listen to what he said, so you don't think that I'm misrepresenting anyone. "We are the true high priestly race of God. Even as God himself bears witness, saying that in every place, among the Gentiles, sacrifices are presented to him, well pleasing and pure. God does not receive sacrifices from anyone except through his priests. I mean those offered by the Christians, in every region of the Earth, with the thanksgiving of the bread and of the cup, bearing witness that they are well pleasing to him."

Do you find Paul telling Timothy and Titus to offer sacrifice as part of their ministerial duties? They are exhorted to give themselves to reading, to exhortation, to doctrine (1 Tim. 4:13). They are told how to conduct themselves in the house of God (1 Tim. 3:15). They are told how to govern their families. They are told to preach the Word, be it in season, out of season. "Reprove, rebuke, exhort with all long suffering, and doctrine" (1 Tim. 4:2). However, there is not one word about offering sacrifice.

In the Book of Acts, churches are founded, sinners saved—and that's a beautiful word, "saved." Nothing wrong with it. I know Romanists and apostate Protestants, they make fun of that word, but that's a good Bible word. In the early Church, in the Book of Acts, for example, which covers maybe about forty years or so—that's inspired Church history, and that's where we need to go—not to what is known as ecclesiastical history. But in the Book of Acts, churches are founded, sinners saved, miracles performed, but nowhere do we find anything resembling the so-called sacrifice of the Mass both for the living—and mind you, for the dead. Paul, Silas, Peter, and John never offered Mass in Jerusalem or Antioch. Roman Catholicism is not the system which the apostles preached, for we read nowhere in their inspired record of such a service as the Romish Mass. Roman Catholic priests not only usurp an office that belongs to Jesus Christ, and him alone, but they are without authority, from the Scripture, to offer sacrifice today because the

29

word of God absolutely disproves the existence of a literal sacrifice. The Bible is dogmatic about the fact that there is but one sacrifice.

Arthur W. Pink was correct when he said that Hebrews is the death knell of Roman Catholicism. Chapters 7-10 make it clear that there is one Calvary and not many Masses. Romanism is very clever, being the religious harlot she is. She says there is one Calvary, yes, but many Masses. No, that conflicts with God's word, the Bible. You see, the word "once," or "once for all," is found in those great, classical chapters about nine or ten times. And that word once, once for all, speaks to the finality, the sufficiency of what Jesus did on Calvary's tree. He offered himself a recompense for you and me. He offered up his life to God on behalf of sinners. This offering was absolutely perfect and complete. In other words, nothing can be added to it. This is why the Roman Catholic Mass is useless. It's futile, unnecessary, unscriptural, and un-Christian. Not only is the Mass idolatrist. (By the way, you may think I enjoy saying some of these things tonight, I do not, but they must be said.) Not only is the Mass idolatrist; the Mass is pagan. And if you don't think so, you don't know your Bible. The Bible says that Christ by one offering perfected, forever, them that are sanctified. There is now no more offering for sin.

Christ's offering of himself was a work so perfect, so complete, so sufficient, so efficacious that it needed not to be repeated. It cannot be repeated because in order to be efficacious, Christ must suffer. He has declared that without shedding of blood there is no remission and, hence, that if the offering of Christ had to be repeated, Christ must need have suffered often. Holy Writ makes it clear that to the true Christians, that there is but one sacrifice.

The Church of the popes asserts that the sacrifice of the Mass was instituted at the Last Supper and that whenever this was observed, Christ was offered in a true, proper, and propitiatory sacrifice. Now, to accept this notion is to say that Christ must had been offered thousands of times, between the institution of the ordinance or sacrament and the publication of the epistle to the Hebrews. Now, think about that, really. This false idea is destroyed by the following text: "This he did once when he offered up himself" (Heb. 7:27). I believe this great truth is repeated by the apostle as to warn of a future

Romish, papal rite known as the Mass. "Just as man once dies, so Christ was once offered"—such language is irreconcilable with the theory of Christ's continued sacrifice in the Roman Catholic Mass.

The very repetition of the Jewish sacrifices is evidence their insufficiency. The Roman Catholic Masses are constantly repeated. If the Roman Catholic Mass had been true, Christ had then been offered thousands of times. Catholicism teaches that Christ is unbloodily offered in the Mass. If so, there can be no remission of sin connected with that sacrifice because the Bible says, "Without shedding of blood is no remission" (Heb. 9:22). Yes, the Mass is a diabolical invention, an insult to the all-sufficient work of my Savior on Calvary's tree. To accept the Romish Mass is to impugn, to question, to attack, to deny, to confound the holy character of Jesus who declared, "It is finished" (John 19:30).

There can be no Mass because there is no dogma of Transubstantiation. Supposedly, the priest, by virtue of ordination, is given the power to change or convert bread and wine into Jesus Christ. He has the power to produce divinity, to make God out of mere matter. Isn't that something? It makes me shudder, beloved.

Have you heard of Jean Vianney, a very well-known Roman Catholic saint from France? This is what he said: "Without the priest, the death and passion of our Lord would be of no avail to us." Isn't that something? See the power of the priest! By one word from his lips, he changes a piece of bread into God—a greater feat than the creation of the world. Folks, that is heresy, that is blasphemy, and that hurts the heart of God. So serious is Romanism about this idea that there are curses for those who deny that the priest can convert or change bread and wine into the real body and blood, soul and divinity, bone and marrow of the Lord Jesus Christ. She, Rome, has a curse for him who denies the miraculous conversion of bread and wine into Jesus Christ. Even if the consecrated bread be severed into a thousand parts or into a million crumbs, each part or crumb is the entire Christ. If the wine be divided into drops, too many to number, each drop is the entire Christ. She, Rome, has a curse for him who denies this pagan, superstitious, medieval belief that has no root in God's word, the Bible.

But this is not all. The Church of Rome says that the host or wafer—they call it the host; some of us call it the "wafer God"; some call it the "dough God"—Rome says that the wafer, once it is consecrated, is to be worshipped with the worship of *latria*. I don't know what that is. That's Greek or Latin. I guess I should know, but anyway, it's not English. But it means that the wafer is to receive divine worship. Isn't that something? And Canon VI of the Council Trent says there's a curse for those who deny that particular teaching. How sad to think that our Roman Catholic friends worship a god of flour and water!

Some of Rome's most illustrious theologians hold that Transubstantiation is not found in the New Testament. I find this very interesting. I never knew that, during my twelve years of study for the priesthood. In fact, I've spoken with Roman Catholic priests who deny the dogma of Transubstantiation. One belongs to a very well-known cathedral, in this part of the country, in this state. I suppose he's taking stipends or donations for offering the Mass. But he told me, at least, "Bart, I don't accept Transubstantiation." And there are thousands, perhaps millions of Catholic people who reject that superstitious belief, and yet they profess to be Roman Catholic. I find that very hypocritical and unethical. But—and this should make us grieve—tonight, there are millions of Catholic people who really believe that the priest has that kind of power, to change bread and wine into the Lord Jesus Christ.

You see, beloved, one of the most superficial arguments used by the Church of Rome to promote what is known as the Holy Eucharist is from John 6:53–56. This passage has no connection whatsoever with the Lord's Supper. This discourse was given at least thirteen months before the institution of the Lord's Supper. This is evident from the fact that two Passovers elapsed between the delivery of these words and the institution of the ordinance, which by the way is not a sacrifice. And you can compare John 6:4 with John 12:1. Our Lord uses the present tense, "Except ye eat." It was their responsibility to partake of that spiritual food, even at the time when he delivered the discourse. Therefore the words cannot refer to the sacrament. I don't like that word "sacrament" anyway. It doesn't refer to the ordinance, which was not then instituted. Common sense dictates that this passage be taken figuratively. It refers to the one way of salvation, by faith.

I believe verse 53 is the key to the proper, correct interpretation of this chapter or the proper understanding of this chapter. It says, "He that cometh to me shall never hunger, and he that believeth on me shall never thirst." How are we to feed on Christ? By coming to him. How are we to drink His blood? By believing on him. And then verse 63: "It is the spirit that quickeneth. The flesh profiteth nothing. The words that I speak unto you, they are spirit, and they are life." Christ constantly employed figurative language in order to enforce the truth.

The apostles understood our Lord correctly. They didn't twist the word of God. They were accustomed to figurative language, in which the Savior always spoke. They understood that the words "this Passover" did not mean the literal Passover. And likewise, the words "This is my body" did not mean the literal body but the commemoration of it. They did not believe that Christ, whom they saw, and with whom they spoke, took his own body in his own hands and broke it into twelve parts, each part being a whole body, and gave his flesh and blood to them to eat or consume. It was contrary to God's law to drink blood. And much more, human blood. The words "Do this in remembrance of me" and the apostolic declaration "For as often as ye eat this bread and drink this cup, ye do show the Lord's death till He comes" prove that this ordinance commemorates the Savior who is bodily absent. You get that? How could it be done in remembrance of him if he were present in body, soul, blood, and deity? How could it be said that we show the Lord's death till he come, if he were already come, literally, upon the Romish altar?

Paul calls the elements the bread and the cup. "For as often as ye eat this bread and drink this cup" and "so let him eat of that bread and drink of that cup" (1 Cor. 11:26-28). Note that the Church of Rome does not receive this passage in a literal sense but in a non-natural sense. "After the same manner, also he took the cup when he had supped saying, 'This cup is the New Testament in my blood. This do ye as oft as ye drink it in remembrance of me. For as often as you eat this bread and drink this cup, ye do show the Lord's death till he come" (1 Cor. 11:23–26). Christ said, "This cup is the New Testament." Was the cup literally changed into the New Testament? He did not say or mean that the cup was literally the New Testament. Therefore, he did not mean that the bread was literally his body. To insist upon a hyper-interpretation, to insist upon a literal interpretation, is contrary to common sense and to the practice of Roman Catholicism in other respects.

A well-known Catholic theologian of yesteryear, Karl Adam, in his book *The Spirit of Catholicism,* writes, "We Catholics acknowledge, readily, without any shame, nay with pride, that Catholicism cannot be identified simply and wholly with primitive Christianity, nor even the Gospel of Christ." I'm quoting a Roman Catholic author. He is right. Romanism is a subtle departure from historic, biblical, fundamental, evangelical Christianity. The study of Roman Catholicism, superficially, may lead one to think that the Roman Catholic Church is Christian. Perhaps it was founded by Jesus Christ. After all, she believes that Jesus Christ is the Incarnate Son of God. His Virgin Birth, his miracles, his substitutionary work on the Cross, his Resurrection, Ascension, and Second Coming. These are official Roman Catholic teachings. However, these truths, which she has, have been distorted, nullified by her poisonous doctrines.

The sixteenth-century Reformers said that Roman Catholicism is apostate, not because of a denial of truth but because of additions which become a departure from it. There is an Italian expression, and it goes like this: *"Roma veduta, fede perduta."* Rome seen, faith lost. It should read, "When Catholic Rome is seen and studied, all faith in Romanism is lost."

Now, my friend Mr. Keating and I agree that there must be a rule by which we can know divine truth. I mean there has got to be something to go by, to test Christianity. However, the Romanist has one rule and the Christian another. The differences are not only in certain doctrines but also in what constitutes a basis of authority.

It is no secret that the Church of Rome promotes Scripture and Tradition. Dr. Charles Berry, a personal friend of mine, a former Augustinian priest and professor, was told in the seminary that placing authority only in the Bible is comparable to being in a row boat with one oar. You've got to have two oars, the Bible and Tradition. The Council of Trent accepted the Bible and Tradition. Cardinal Robert Bellarmine said that the Bible is useful for the

Church but not necessary. How do you like that? Cardinal Stanislaus Hosius said, "It would have been a better situation for the Church if no Scripture at all had ever existed." In France the reading of the Bible was forbidden by the Council of Toulouse in 1229. The next year its translation was forbidden at the Council of Rheims. Its translation was forbidden for the French people. The papal bull known as *Unigenitus*, in 1713, condemned the proposition that "the reading of the Holy Scripture is for all."

I realize that things are somewhat different because of Vatican II, but, again, we don't want to be naïve. I believe the changes are cosmetic, superficial, and minor. I realize that Catholicism today is promoting Bible studies or biblical studies. However, I don't believe it's genuine. As long as the Church of Rome will unite the Word of God with humanistic tradition, I believe that hurts the heart of God. I believe God hates that, that is compromise. Right away, the Roman Catholic will appeal to the Word of God to support Tradition. Isn't that something? That really fascinates me. The Roman Catholic really doesn't believe that the Bible is the final authority. And yet, the Romanist will go to the Scripture to support Tradition. And here is a classic example: I heard my friend Karl use John 20:30. "And many other signs truly did Jesus in the presence of his disciples which are not written in this book." Surely, no one here tonight will deny that much of what Jesus did is not written. But what is written is sufficient, for the next verse reads, "But these are written that ye might believe that Jesus is the Christ, the son of God, and that believing, ye might have life through his name" (John 20:31).

Of course, Rome doesn't like to think that Tradition is extra-biblical revelation. Maybe not in theory, but in practice, it is. But I heard—I think Karl mentioned tonight, 2 Thessalonians 2:15: "Stand fast and hold the traditions which ye have been taught whether by word or our epistle." It's amazing. In my day as a Catholic we would use that text, out of context, and the same old Roman Catholic recipes are still being projected, at precious people who have been seduced with another gospel.

Second Thessalonians 2:15, right here in this text, there is no distinction between oral tradition and written tradition. We will not deny that what is found in the Bible was first taught by word. You and I would not deny that.

But we believe that all of what was necessary for salvation and the teaching of Christ and his apostles is committed to writing, by the inspiration of the Holy Spirit. And were the apostles alive now we would receive, with humility and obedience, their word, whether delivered orally or by writing, wouldn't we? If the Church of Rome can only prove it, why don't they prove it? No Roman Catholic priest, in all these years, has made any attempt to show this Judas priest this point, namely, that her Tradition is apostolic. If only they will prove that their traditions are apostolic, we will receive them. But this they cannot do. The Scripture alone is what the apostles taught.

When Paul wrote to Timothy to keep that which was committed to his trust, he was not advocating the Bible plus but rather the necessity of adhering to the teaching of the apostles. "Who can deny that there were many things said and done by Christ and his apostles which are not written, for the world, itself, could not contain the books that should be written" (John 21:25). But sufficient is what is recorded. "But these are written that ye might believe that Jesus is the Christ, the Son of God and that believing ye might have life though his name" (John 20:31). The burden of proof is with Rome to show that her traditions are apostolic.

Catholicism teaches that Tradition was first oral though later on written down by Church Fathers. Boy, the Church Fathers have a high place of prominence in the Church of Rome. Why, I do not know. The early Christians wrote little because they lived in a time of severe persecution. What is found in the writings of the Church Fathers in the second and third centuries has little reference to doctrines disputed between Christians and Roman Catholics today. Therefore, Tradition for hundreds of years was nothing more than mere report, and this is what Rome receives with equal reverence. Isn't that something? As the written word of God, we cannot build our faith on mere report. This makes for a very insecure foundation.

Moreover, beloved, the Church Fathers contradict each other. Some of the Church Fathers of the second century believed in the personal reign of Jesus Christ, some did not. Some believed in images, some did not. Some accepted the canonicity of the apocryphal or spurious books, and some did not. And so there was no unanimity. There was no unanimous consent among the early Christian writers. Rome can never prove that her Traditions are divine and apostolic. Not only is Rome's authority in the Scripture and in Tradition but in the Church. What really has weight is not so much the Bible and Tradition but what is known as the teaching authority or the Magisterium. For the Catholic, be he cleric or lay member, it's simple obedience to the pope, more than anything else. That's really the bottom line. You see, the Roman Catholic religion refers to herself as infallible, but the question tonight is this: where is this infallible authority? Is it only in the pope, when he speaks *ex cathedra*? Is it in Church councils or in Church councils with the pope as head? Catholics are divided on this matter.

When all is said and done, the attribute of infallibility is said to belong to the assembly of a few bishops and theological experts, with the pope at their head. Frankly, beloved, I find nothing in the Bible about a man being infallible, and there is nothing in divine revelation about an infallible church, when it comes to biblical interpretation. What infallible authority has declared that Romanism is infallible? There is none. Rome argues that without the authority of the Roman Church we cannot prove the genuineness and authenticity and inspiration of the Bible. I remember that at lunch last winter Karl used that very fallacious argument. If the authority for Scripture rests in a few pontificating clerics, then the truth of the Bible rests on a shaky, sandy foundation.

In proof of papal infallibility, the Catholic hierarchy likes to go to Matthew 16:18: "Thou art Peter and upon this rock I will build my church, and the gates of hell shall not prevail against it." And then verse 19: "I will give unto thee the keys to the kingdom of heaven." Now, I know Mr. Keating does not go along with the distinction we have in the Greek between the Greek *petros*, which means a shifting, insecure rock, and *petra*, which refers to a solid, immovable rock. I think this distinction points to the fact that Christ was actually speaking in Greek, not Aramaic. Right now I can just hear one say, "Oh, let's not quibble about the Greek. Let's not quibble about the Greek gender endings because our Lord did not speak in Greek but in Aramaic. Well, I don't believe this helps the person that takes that position. Matthew gave the account of the incident and quotes Jesus directly. Matthew could have quoted it, "Thou art *petros* and upon this *petros* I will build my Church," but he did not. He quoted it, "Thou art *petros*, and upon this *petra*, I will build my Church." Matthew could have used the same word, but he did not, beloved.

The Roman Catholic officials, in an effort to escape the force of this argument, say, "There is no use quibbling about the Greek. Our Lord did not speak in Greek." But wait a minute. Matthew reports it in Greek. Do you not believe that Matthew was inspired? Why discredit Matthew and this account? All this just in an effort to try to uphold the primacy of Peter. Friends, do you not know that Jesus promised to send the apostles the Holy Spirit? That included Matthew. He promised to lead them into all truth. That also included Matthew. Why discredit Matthew's record? Besides, if you do your homework from Roman Catholic sources, you will see that they accept Greek as one of the original biblical languages. Shame on the Church of Rome for saying that it makes no difference how Matthew wrote it. Do you not have any respect for the correctness and inspiration of Matthew's Gospel? Maybe you do. But if you say Christ didn't write in Greek, it was Aramaic, then you show that you have no regard, whatsoever, for Matthew.

Now folks, do me a favor tonight, before you leave. I know it's getting late. And, listen, I appreciate your patience very much. Tell me, what commentaries written during the first thousand years of Christianity mention the primacy or the papacy? Not one mentions the primacy of the Bishop of Rome. I was really surprised to hear Karl start off with the idea of Peter being in Rome. I was quite surprised to see that he would go that direction, but I believe there is no commentary, whatsoever, written by some well-known Roman Catholic authority on this particular verse. Such an idea and interpretation did not even exist as a heresy, namely the primacy of Peter. God obviously knew that centuries later that the Roman Catholic system would seriously distort the position of Peter the apostle. He inspired Isaiah, in Hebrew, to write this: "And you are my witnesses. Is there any god besides me? Or is there any other rock? I know of none" (Isaiah 44:8). The word "rock" is an emblem of deity. Isn't that precious? And there is no other god, and there is no other rock. If you say that there can be another rock, you would exegetically have to admit the possibility of another god.

That's right. If the apostles believed that no longer would God be perceived as the only rock, then why did not they ask how a human could be described in terms of an Old Testament emblem of deity? If they entertained the notion that Peter was the rock, to the Jewish mind it would have seemed that Peter also was God. What did it mean to the original apostles at the time this was spoken, Matthew 16:18–19? Why did they wonder how it applied to Peter? Why did they not wonder why Peter fell so hard when he denied the Lord and forsook him? Why didn't they ever, in the New Testament, ask Peter to settle any disputes? Why did the apostles wonder who was the greatest among them, if they interpreted Peter as being the rock upon which the Church was built?

Folks, in connection with papal supremacy, Peter was not a priest. He was not a pope, and I don't believe he ever got to Rome, and if he did, so what? But he was not the rock. He was not the rock. Why do we want to take that away from Jesus? The pope is not the rock, but what does this section, Matthew 16:18-19, have to do with the dogma that certain Roman Catholic clergymen in council, convened by the pope, are infallible? Is there a word in this text about pope, council, or Roman Church? There is not. Romanism was not even in existence. And it was in Antioch that the disciples were first called Christians. Isn't that right?

The theories of certain Roman Catholic theologians concerning Matthew 16:18-19 afford a remarkable example of division in a so-called infallible community. While Bonaventure and Liguori and others teach that the pope is infallible, still others deny this doctrine. Did you know that? Dr. Ignaz von Döllinger was a very famous priest, a historian from Munich, in the nineteenth century, and this is what he said: "Even the boldest champions of papal absolutism assumed that the popes could err, and that their decisions were no certain criterion."

Have you heard of Pope Pius IX? I read something interesting lately. I read that there is an effort underway to canonize him as a Roman Catholic saint. Now, he had three girlfriends. Don't be upset. What do you expect of an unregenerate? You see that's no worse than religious idolatry. That's no worse than promoting salvation by works. Pope Pius IX, during Vatican I, made the provision that in case he were to die during the Council, its decisions would take precedence over the decisions made by previous council or popes and thus correct any inconsistencies there might be. If the pope were truly the vicar of Christ, beloved, would he dare to make provisions for contradictions?

Think about it. If the doctrine of infallibility were defined by Christ, or by any apostle, why did the Roman Catholic institution wait until 1870 to make this doctrine a dogma of the Romanists, binding under pain of mortal sin? There is a curse for the Roman Catholic who rejects the infallibility of the pope when he speaks from his chair. Why did the Church of Rome wait for centuries to define it? The truth is that papal infallibility was not generally taught until 1870. If the popes are infallible only since 1870, what were they before that time? And if they were fallible before 1870, what about their doctrine?

A year after the pope was declared infallible, the *Catholic World*, a very well-known Catholic publication, stated, "We have no right to ask reasons of the Church, any more than of Almighty God, as a preliminary to our submission. We are to take with unquestioning docility whatever instruction the Church gives," August 1871, page 598. Paul said, "These were more noble than those in Thessalonica and that they received the word with all readiness of mind and search the scriptures daily, whether those things were so." The Bereans took the Bible as their guide, and Paul commended them for doing so. The Bible, not the pope, is the safe guide. The doctrine of infallibility came gradually into the Roman system, like many of her doctrines.

I heard my friend Karl Keating mention the development of doctrine. That came about with Cardinal Newman. He was an Anglican priest that later on converted to Romanism. He became a Cardinal. Now there is an effort to canonize him as a Roman Catholic saint. My, that will bring a lot of Episcopalians and Anglicans into the Church of Rome.

Did someone say, Amen? If you did, you need to repent. Now let me say this, beloved. Let me say this. Let me say this very quickly. The Bible says, "Let no man deceive you, by any means." No wonder the New Testament constantly warns, "Be not deceived." We are told, "Believe not every spirit, but try the spirits whether they are of God, because many false prophets are going out into the world. This means that the teachings of all churches must come under the test of God's word, the Holy Scripture, because there are false apostles, deceitful workers, transforming themselves into the apostles of Christ. It is no marvel for Satan himself is transformed into an angel of light. Therefore it is no great thing if his ministers also be transformed as the ministers of righteousness whose end shall be according to their works. Now we have seen that neither Tradition nor the Roman Catholic Church is the rule of faith. I want to show that the Bible is the only objective source of divine revelation. In Old Testament times, the written law was the rule of the people. And if you don't think so, all you have to do is look at Deuteronomy 6:6-9. And then look in Deuteronomy 6—

[Interruptions from the audience, followed by consultation with the moderator.]

Folks, I believe in submission, obedience to my moderator. He said I've gone long over the time. I'd like to mention the fact that originally it was to be 30 minutes, and then Karl and I agreed to have it for 45, but I understood that we were to be flexible when it came to the presentation, so I will have to yield to the moderator at this time. Thank you so very much.

KEATING: Bart and I didn't make any arrangements for rebuttals of each other, but there are a few things that I just cannot let pass in what he said. I feel like a man who has been commanded to unravel a bowl of spaghetti, and he's been given one chopstick. There are so many incorrect things in what Bart said. Now, his Bible quotations were accurate, but don't you think that the Catholic Church, which preserved the Bible through nineteen centuries, might realize that those quotations were in it? If you think that the Catholic Church was all powerful in the Middle Ages, why wasn't it smart enough to destroy all the Bibles? Why did it preserve them in monasteries? But let me get to some of his points. I want to mention just three things, and then we'll take questions, so I for one won't go an extra 45 minutes. Let me go backwards in sequence here.

First, what is this business about Pope Pius IX in the nineteenth century having three girlfriends? There is a very interesting book called *No Popery*. It's by Fr. Herbert Thurston, S.J. About half the book is devoted to calumnies against Pius IX. When he died he left what he owned, which was the value of a few hundred dollars today, to widowed sisters of his, who had no pension or other income. Anti-Catholics transformed his sisters into women unrelated to him, and the amount left as not being his few personal possessions but the great wealth of the Church. That's ridiculous.

Second, Matthew 16:18. Bart skirted around the matter. We know that Matthew in fact was written in Aramaic because the earliest writings we have talking about the writing of that Gospel can be found in Eusebius, the first Church historian, writing around 325. He said, "Matthew wrote in the common language of the Hebrew people." That was Aramaic. That's what people spoke. On the Cross, Jesus spoke Aramaic. "*Eloi, Eloi, lama sabachthani.*" Aramaic is still spoken today in the Mass in some Eastern Catholic Churches. In Matthew 16:18, in the Aramaic, the phrase would have been, "Thou art *kepha*, and upon this *kepha*, I will build my Church."

The play on words there is obvious. In translating Matthew's Aramaic to Greek you change *kepha*, which means rock, big rock, into *petra*. Quite true. You cannot use *petra*, though, as a man's name because in Greek nouns have gender endings. *Petra* is a feminine noun. You can't use it as a man's name. You have to change the ending to a masculine ending, so you get *petros*. The only way you can translate the Aramaic into Greek would have been "Thou art *petros* and upon this *petra* I will build my Church." French translations have a parallel to the Aramaic. The word in French for rock is *pierre*. In French the Bibles read, "Thou art *pierre*, and upon this *pierre*, I will build my Church." I mean the play on words is just too obvious, but most Fundamentalists ignore that and look at just the Greek as though it proves something. It doesn't.

The third point I want to mention is another historical blunder. Someone over here gave me a few amens a few moments ago when I mentioned that the Church made no attempt to wipe out the Bible. The guy said, "Oh, yes it did." Bart had mentioned the Council of Toulouse in 1229. Toulouse is in

France. He also mentioned a council at Rheims. He said those councils banned the Bible. That's true. But do you know why they banned the Bible? Let's say your son or your daughter brings home a Bible, say the King James Version, into which somebody has pasted un-Christian lines, maybe pornographic pictures. Would you ban that Bible from your children? Of course you would. You'd say, "The only Bible, my son or daughter, that you're authorized by your parents to use is an unadulterated Bible, which I encourage you to use. But not this one with a false translation or other things added in."

In the early thirteenth century, in southern France, there was a heresy called Albigensianism, also known as Catharism. Fundamentalists often like to picture Albigensianism as a Middle Ages version of Fundamentalism. Why? Because the Albigensianism wanted the Bible not in Latin but in the vernacular, French. The Albigensians, under either Catholic or Fundamentalist standards, were no Christians at all. They were Manichees. They thought there was a war between the spirit and the body, in such a way that marriage was immoral. They recognized that people have instincts, so they approved of concubines. They let that go by, but they would not approve of marriage because the authorities would be okaying the union of a man and a woman. The Albigensians had a sacrament, somewhat like baptism. (They didn't believe in baptism.) They had something called *consolamentum.* you got it once in your life. After that, if you committed any sin, you could not go to heaven. People tried to arrange the *consolamentum* to be given on their deathbeds. Sometimes things didn't work out right. Sometimes people recovered, after getting the *consolamentum.* Then you got to undergo what was called the *endura,* endurance, which was forced suicide. You had your choice. Either you could be suffocated with a pillow by the church elders, or they would withhold food from you until you died. It was one or the other. The reason the Albigensian church was attacked by the Catholic Church was because those are immoral doctrines, and Albigensianism was disrupting society in France.

You don't have to accept my word for it. Why don't you turn to a reputable (from Fundamentalists point of view) Protestant scholar on the Middle Ages, H. C. Lea, who was an American? He was very anti-Catholic, but in his book on the Inquisition he wrote about the Albigensians. He said that, had Albigensianism prevailed in Europe, Christianity and civilization would have been extinguished. He had no misgivings about what was done to the Albigensians. He knew theirs was an evil system.

Now those are just three examples of more than three dozen mistakes (I counted them) that Bart brought out in his talk, and they were seriously mistaken. If he and I duel, armed with decibels, I can't win. He's experienced, with ten years or more as a preacher. I can't win on that basis. I can't yell to a victory. But what you can do is look behind what each of us says. You can get our literature and compare for yourself. Put yourself a step away from the present position you have, whether you're Catholic or Fundamentalist, and take an open view. One thing I ask you though is, please, don't be entirely willing to swallow every negative thing you hear. You know from your own experience, from people you meet who are Catholic, that they aren't all fools. Has it never occurred to you that there is probably more to their religion that you've been told by people who, for whatever reason—personal grudge or whatever—hate the Church?

It would have been easy for me to come here and paint Fundamentalism black. You know very well if you're a Fundamentalist that half the people in America think of you as redneck Bible thumpers. Right. By that they mean that they think you're stupid when in fact that's not the case. Yes, you're going to find stupid people in any religion. You can't deny that, but you don't like that caricature of Fundamentalism. I don't either. I've spoken against it. I've written against it for Catholic audiences. I think that you ought to expect Fundamentalist writers and pundits to do the same when it comes to the Church of Rome. You ought to demand of them a little courtesy, a little charity, a little fair play.

MODERATOR: If you have a logical, sensible question, a reasonable question you want to ask, from either side, feel free to ask it.

SPEAKER: I'd like to address Mr. Keating regarding Peter as the first pope. Do you call Paul a liar? In Galatians, he says that Peter was the apostle to the

Jews and he was the apostle to the Gentiles. Why don't you make Paul the first pope because Peter's headquarters was in Jerusalem?

KEATING: At one time, all the apostles were in Jerusalem. Peter later went to Antioch, around the year 42. Later still he went to Rome. At the time of Christ, Rome had the largest Jewish population of any city in the world, more so than Jerusalem. Peter went to the Jews in Rome and evangelized them. Most Jews did not live in Palestine at the time. Thus there's no contradiction.

MODERATOR: Okay. Yes, sir.

SPEAKER: To Mr. Keating: Do you believe everything that the Catholic Church teaches and its ordinances and laws and doctrines?

KEATING: I think I'm about to be set up for something. Yes. Now what's the next part of your question?

SPEAKER: I asked this question to a Catholic nun, and I ask it to you, and I'd like a biblical answer, not a traditional answer or historical answer. In 1 Timothy 2:1, it says, "I exhort therefore, that first of all, supplications, prayers, intercessions and giving of thanks be made for all men." Then it goes on and says, "For there is one God and one mediator between God and men, the man Christ Jesus." I asked the nun why your Catholic writings say there is only one true Mediatrix and that you can get your prayers answered quicker through Mary than you can through Jesus, and I showed her the writings, and she said her only basis was Tradition. I ask you for a biblical basis for praying through Mary.

KEATING: First of all, will you pray for me for discernment on that? If I ask you, will you pray for me that I might be enlightened in that regard? Yes? Do you violate the Bible by doing that because are you acting as a mediator between me and God? You say, now wait a minute. I'm not violating the Bible. We are commanded by Jesus to pray for one another. Is that right?

SPEAKER: I pray through Jesus to God. He's my mediator.

KEATING: In this church, or wherever you might fellowship, you regularly pray for one another. I pray for my friends, my family, for Bart before I came tonight. I may even pray for him afterwards. In doing that, what am I doing? I am being a mediator. Why doesn't he just pray for himself? There is no contradiction there.

MODERATOR: Yes, sir. In the middle right here, in the blue shirt.

SPEAKER: Mr. Keating, let us assume that Peter is the rock. I don't believe that, but let's just assume it. Can you give me a biblical place in the Bible where it says that Peter had successors and that these successors were infallible?

KEATING: The successors would be logically necessary because Christ said his Church would exist throughout the ages and that the gates of hell would not prevail. Human beings die, so it makes sense that there must be a successor to whom power could be handed on. Now, is there somebody perhaps that would want to address a question to Mr. Brewer?

MODERATOR: I just told Bart, "Nobody wants to ask you anything." In the back, back there.

SPEAKER: My question I would like to address to both speakers. It's just a simple question. Jesus spoke many times of hell, and he talked about what a terrible place it is, and I don't want to go there. I would just like to ask both speakers if they could give me any kind of assurance at all that I don't have to go there?

KEATING: Whether you as an individual will go there, of course, none of us can say. We all hope not. We all have a chance of going there. We all have a chance of ruining our lives through sin and ending up there, but whether we go there or not depends upon whether we're supernaturally alive when we die.

If we're supernaturally dead, which we become by turning our backs on God through sin, we will not go there because we'll be unclean and nothing unclean can enter heaven. On the other hand, if we're supernaturally alive, we will go to heaven.

BREWER: Well, contrary to what Mr. Keating said, the Bible indeed is a sufficient source of revelation from cover to cover. To say it's not sufficient is to imply it's deficient. To imply that it's deficient is to indict God's divine sovereignty and folks, that's very serious. So the Bible's the complete revelation from cover to cover. For example, I like to share this information with you. If Scripture were not sufficient for its end, informing us of the saving purposes of God, it could not stand as our sole authority. So when you have a defective view of Scripture, you do not accept the premise that the Bible is a sufficient revelation from cover to cover. Now, when one accepts the Scripture as a complete objective revelation from cover to cover, as that person gets into the Word of God, he will understand that Christ not only saves, but also he keeps. And there—you can only be born again one time. Justification by faith is a one-time act. It's really sad that Romanism promotes processed salvation. You're born again, born again, born again. That is heresy.

SPEAKER: How do you get saved?

BREWER: How does a person get saved? Well, the Bible makes it very clear, by repenting and receiving Christ as Lord and Savior. That's not a flippant, quick decision for Christ. That means standing upon the completed work of Christ. Another way to explain it would be to exchange your own righteousness for the righteousness of Jesus, and we have that example in Romans 4, the example of Abraham: "To him that worketh not, but believeth on him that justifieth the ungodly, his faith is counted for righteousness," and yet the Church of Rome places sanctifying grace in sacraments.

Now I think what is very unfortunate is that sometimes a Roman Catholic apologist either deliberately, or perhaps not so deliberately, will not give you the whole picture. I remember as a Roman Catholic priest when prospective converts came to the office we were told to speak to them about the simplicity of the faith. That meant keeping the person away from the facts. I think Mr. Keating has done that very well tonight. He has not given us an in-depth picture of Romanism.

MODERATOR: Lady in the yellow blouse. Right there.

SPEAKER: I wanted to ask Mr. Brewer: I've been a Catholic all my life, and I've never heard as much hate spewed. Why are you so anti-Catholic? We have a lot of things that aren't in the Bible that we believe by faith. We have faith in the things that we believe to be true because we want to believe them. I don't care what you believe, but I don't denigrate you. As for your faith, whatever it is you have, methinks you protest too much. You were a priest. I wonder if you weren't just sorry that you couldn't cut the mustard.

BREWER: Thank you very much. I really need to apologize because before getting started, I should have mentioned that we love the Catholic, but we cannot support the teachings.

Have you ever heard of Augustine? He said that we are to hate error and love the man, and that is my position. Paul said, "Speak the truth in love." When Paul wrote to the Galatians, he asked, "Am I your enemy because I tell you the truth?" So tonight, we're not attacking you but a system that seduces people with another gospel.

MODERATOR: All right, over here, young man.

SPEAKER: I would like to address a question to Rev. Brewer to the point about the divisions in doctrine among Protestants, people that accept Scripture alone. Some Protestants believe that once one has entered the state of grace, he can never be lost again. Other Protestants believe one can be lost after he has entered the state of grace. Some Protestants such as the Lutherans accept the doctrine of the Real Presence. Other Protestants, such as Baptists, don't. What's your thought on that?

BREWER: Well, apparently, I have said too much already, so let me mention this, that had you been truly born again the Bible way and had you really understood the Scripture, you would not had been a convert to the Church of Rome. May I just say in short that, technically speaking, we are not Protestant. I recognize the Reformation movement as a valid movement, but technically speaking, we are not Protestant. In other words, we're not out of the Reformation of the sixteenth century. We stand upon the infallible word of God, and once you really study our Lord's attitude toward the Scripture, you will see that salvation is only by faith.

MODERATOR: This lady right here.

SPEAKER: I'd like to address this to Mr. Brewer: Why did you leave the Church? Is there a particular event or reason that you could give? You noted at the beginning of your address that we could just look at the Bible and see the clear meaning of it, yet throughout your presentation I think we were given your interpretation of the Bible. As this gentlemen's question was just referring to, whose interpretation are we to take as authentic? Are we to take yours, or are we to take his, or are we to take mine? How do we discern what is the clear interpretation because obviously you don't believe what I believe about the Bible?

BREWER: As I tried to say earlier, we're not dealing with interpretation tonight, but the plain facts of God's word. And once you understand that the Bible is authoritative, then you will accept its inspiration and inerrancy as the final court of appeal.

Why did I leave the Roman Catholic priesthood? There were two teachings during my time in the chaplaincy with the Marines that I started to question. Number one: celibacy. I believe celibacy makes many a priest a professional hypocrite. Mandatory celibacy has no support from the Bible. Optional celibacy, yes. Mandatory celibacy, no. Paul in writing to Timothy and Titus gives the requirements for an individual who has a calling to preach the gospel. The second teaching I started to question—and believe me, it was with fear and trembling—

was sacramental confession. If you and I will take the totality of Scripture, we see indeed that no one can forgive sin. Christ died for past, present, and future sin. I dare say that sacramental confession is one of the great sources of immorality. It is unnatural for a male or female to confess sin to a priest.

MODERATOR: Okay. This man right here in the middle. Yes, sir.

SPEAKER: I see on one side Mr. Brewer is saying that we are to rely on Scripture and Scripture alone. And on this side, you're saying, Mr. Keating, that we are to rely on the Scripture as long as it doesn't deviate from Tradition. Is that correct?

KEATING: The Catholic position is that Scripture and Tradition are the twin sources of revelation. They don't conflict, and Scripture is properly thought of as a part of the oral tradition under which Christianity was first passed down. If Scripture was never written, Christianity would still exist. The truths would still be there, but they would have been passed down orally. When you look at the Bible, you see the one thing the Bible is not is a theological treatise or catechism. In the New Testament you have four biographies, a partial history book, which is also a travelogue, and letters to individuals and to small communities. All of those presume that the people to whom they were written were already Christians. The Bible was not written for non-Christians so they could learn what the religion is about. The Bible needs to be supplemented by the full truth that Christ left to the apostles.

MODERATOR: All the way in the back, back there.

SPEAKER: Yes, I'd like to address this to both men. I believe all of us here realize that there is no way to get in to heaven if man has sin in his life. How then, biblically, is sin purged?

BREWER: We have to remember the word "substitution." That's why there's no Roman Catholic Mass. Christ took your place on the Cross. He paid the price of sin. He purged your sin and my sin on the Cross. When a person repents, that's when justification by faith takes place. That simply means that one is acquitted of the charge of sin. Christ died for the ungodly. He died for the unrighteous. He came to die for sinners, so that's how sin is forgiven.

KEATING: Actually, I have nothing to contradict what Bart said. I would just add that our Lord, as he was leaving, left us means through which we are able to make sure that, in fact, our sins are forgiven. You know it's very easy for any of us to go into our room to pray and say, "I'm sure that my contrition is adequate enough that God must have forgiven me." Sin has a social nature. Christ understands that. He instituted the sacraments, one of which was confession. Christ instituted that sacrament so that we can be sure that our sins are forgiven.

SPEAKER: I'm asking primarily what the Catholic Church teaches on purgatory.

BREWER: Is this for me or Karl? Purgatory simply is this, if you're not good enough to go to heaven, bad enough to go to hell, there's an intermediate place where you atone for sin. However, again, the Bible makes it very clear that Christ died for past, present, and future sin. There's only one propitiation for sin, and that's why in Hebrews 1:3 it says that by himself he purged our sin. You really have to examine the evolution of Roman Catholic teaching to see that this teaching absolutely has no foundation at all in the Bible. You talk about exploiting people, that's exactly what purgatory is all about.

KEATING: Two scriptural points immediately come to mind. One is that nothing unclean shall enter heaven. Most of us when we die are not going to be perfectly clean. The second is from 2 Maccabees: "It's a holy and wholesome thought to pray for the dead." Protestants don't accept 2 Maccabees and some other books in the Catholic Bible as part of Scripture, and the reason, largely, is that the Reformers threw them out precisely because they uphold some Catholic doctrines. The official teachings of the Church as to what books belong to the Bible go all the way back to the Council of Carthage in the last decade of the fourth century. That council included Maccabees as part of the Bible. Now if you want to pick and choose what you will accept as the Bible, that's up to you. All I'm saying is that the Catholic Church looks at the whole Bible, not just the parts that it finds conducive to its preferred doctrines.

One thing that I didn't get to bring up before, and I was going to mention when Bart was answering an earlier question, was this: most people, including all Fundamentalists, think that Fundamentalists get their doctrines by reading the Bible. Incorrect. They start with pre-existing doctrines that are substantiated as well as they can be by going to the Bible and looking for things that seem to substantiate them. You may say no, no, no. But I suspect there's not a one of you who once had no feel for the Bible at all, had never seen it, had no religious position whatever, and opened the Bible and said, "Oh, I can see that all this shows the Fundamentalist position." You learned the Fundamentalist position, and through your learning of it you found certain arguments from Scripture that seem to support it.

MODERATOR: This young man is standing up already.

SPEAKER: Yeah, I'd like to address this to both of you. What does the Bible say concerning infant baptism and in the context of salvation? I realize the Catholic Church, from my upbringing, has taught that infant baptism has something to do with the salvation of that child. I am an ex-Catholic. I have found that to be totally wrong, and I would like both of your opinions on that.

BREWER: I would not want to give you my opinion. I like to mention what the Bible states with great clarity. You know what there is about infant baptism? Nothing. And baptism is for the believer. You know, I had to swallow my religious pride one day, realizing that there is no salvation in baptism. That's one of the great heresies propagated by the Church of Rome. There is nothing in the Bible about infant baptism.

KEATING: On the infant baptism question, it's not taught directly either way in Scripture. We do find that Paul baptized whole households. Presumably households include children. If you look at the earliest books written by Christians after the New Testament, such as the *Didache* and the writings of Ignatius of Antioch and others, they refer specifically to children and infants, using both words, as being properly baptized. Here's what you have to do. If you reject their understanding of early Christianity, what you have to say is this: during the time some of the apostles were still alive, such John who died at the end of the first century, the great majority of Christians dropped the faith and took up this other stuff. And if that was the case, why are there no writings of that early period which say, "Hey, look at these people! Ignatius of Antioch, Irenaeus, and others, they're contradicting the faith that we had from the apostles"? You find no writings like that in the early history. Early Christians were the most conservative people you can imagine. They had exactly one test to see if a doctrine was acceptable, and the test was this: is it an innovation from what has been handed down from our Fathers in the faith? Nobody in the early centuries disclaimed infant or child baptism.

MODERATOR: Okay, the lady in the purple dress back there.

SPEAKER: This is for Mr. Keating. You mentioned about prayers for the dead. I was wondering how long will I pray for my loved ones who are in purgatory in order for them to get out of it? Do you know?

KEATING: Nobody knows, and the Church has never said that anybody knows. There's no way to know what efficacy any of our prayers have on that issue or anything else. You may pray for the conversion of somebody or for some temporal good. We have no way to measure exactly what the effect of your prayer may be. If you happen to pray for somebody to get to heaven, and let's say the person is already there, your prayers don't go to waste. God doesn't waste your prayers. The goodness of your prayers will be applied to somebody else if necessary.

MODERATOR: Okay. Andy?

SPEAKER: So you believe that's true? If we can work our way to heaven, it's no longer grace. If it's grace, then it's no longer works. Which is which?

KEATING: It's easy, Andy, to make a caricature of anybody's position. Now Bart's made a number of caricatures tonight of the Catholic position. I explained it would be easy for me to do the same for your position. You make a false dichotomy. It's either grace or it's works. God expects us to cooperate with him if we expect to get to heaven. He won't save us in spite of ourselves. He's redeemed us, but if we insist on not going to heaven, he's not going to force us to go there. On the other hand, his grace abounds, and there is grace enough for everybody.

MODERATOR: Okay. The lady back there in the blue sweater. There's two of them. Oh, my.

SPEAKER: I was born and raised a Catholic and I went through twelve years of private school. I was raised to believe that the Bible is the Word of God, even though there was never one in the house, they were nice to have, but not necessary, and none of what I learned was based on it, but I was told that is the Word of God, and now you're saying that it is, but Tradition is important.

KEATING: I'm sorry that as a Catholic you might have received an inadequate education. After all, Bart did. He didn't learn to tell time.

SPEAKER: My inadequate education was that the Bible was the Word of God. Is that inadequate in your eyes?

KEATING: If you weren't given the Bible and didn't get to read the Bible when you were younger, I would call that inadequate. However, you might have also not been paying attention too much at Mass, if you were going to Mass at the time, because in every Mass the Bible is read. You have a reading from the Gospel, for example, and over a three-year liturgical cycle virtually all verses of the Gospels are read aloud. You also get readings from other parts of the New Testament. You get a reading from the psalms and you get a reading from the Old Testament. It's a pity, frankly, that in the last number of decades there was not a great emphasis in Catholic teaching to encourage people to read the Bible. Here I refer to the local level. The popes and the bishops were very adamant that Bible reading was necessary and good, and they encouraged it, but that often didn't trickle down as well as it ought to have. This is one place Catholics can learn something from Fundamentalists who show a real love for the Bible. I see more Catholics taking a love for the Bible, and more Catholics are reading it. That's very good. This sorry state of affairs came up because of the Reformation when a false emphasis given to the Bible by the Protestants and Catholics got scared off. It's too bad that it happened, but it's a historical fact that it did.

SPEAKER: My last question is: how can you justify the wealth of the Vatican, and can you justify the amount of time given to requests for money by the Catholic Church as opposed to what I've seen in other churches?

KEATING: Well, I don't know what you've see in other churches.

SPEAKER: I've seen no requests.

KEATING: For my part, I've seen few requests in Catholic churches, and I've been going to Catholic churches for quite a while, but you asked me to compare specifically money questions. Do you have any feel for what the annual budget of the Vatican might be? It's about the same as the budget for the Archdiocese of Chicago. Aside from subsidizing poor dioceses around the world, the Vatican funds hospitals and orphanages and pays for missionaries in areas where they cannot be supported because the people are too poor. Almost all of the wealth of the Catholic Church consists of artwork, orphanages, hospitals, and church buildings. They've been in the church for centuries. Yes, you could sell it all off, but there wouldn't be enough to run the federal government for more than a few weeks. The wealth isn't as great as you think. St. Peter's is a magnificent building with valuable artwork in it, but there's not a lot of cash flowing around.

SPEAKER: What I'd like to know for both of you is why the Catholic Church has Christ on the cross and why Fundamentalists have Christ off the cross.

BREWER: We believe that Christ is risen, so why have a bloody figure on the cross, which is a crucifix? That stems from Roman Catholic Tradition. I really believe this: once the Catholic becomes born again, the biblical way and begins to have a relationship with Christ and gets grounded in the Scripture, then some of these things gradually dissipate.

KEATING: In this country, most Catholics belong to what we call the Western or Latin rite of the Church. A small minority here, but a majority of Catholics in the Near East, belong to what we call the Eastern rites. In the Latin churches, commonly you'll see Christ crucified. In the Eastern churches, commonly you'll see Christ triumphant. He's on the cross, but he has his arms up in victory. Each one has a certain emphasis. We don't deny that he's risen and is in heaven. The reason that the crucifix with the dying Christ became popular, and particularly in the Middle Ages, was that there was a keen sense of the suffering that Christ went through for us because of our sins. In the East, there was an equally keen sense of the victory he had over death. You can have it either way, and you can have a cross without Christ if you wish, because you'll also find some of those. Each emphasizes something different, but don't make the mistake of saying, "The local Catholic church has Christ crucified, so they must think he never rose from the dead." No Catholic believes that.

MODERATOR: This man in the blue coat.

SPEAKER: Okay. If I'm not mistaken, the popes are celibate. Paul in I Corinthians 9:5 says, "Have we not power to lead about a sister, a wife, as well as other apostles and as brethren of the Lord and Cephas?" The name Cephas refers here to Peter.

KEATING: Catholics have always admitted that some of the early popes were married. We don't know whether during Jesus' ministry Peter's wife still was alive. We know that his mother-in-law was alive because Jesus cured her. So we know that Peter, at least at one time, and maybe still then, was married. Several popes after Peter were married, as were some bishops. Over the centuries, that fell out of habit. It was decided that it was wiser for bishops to be celibate, which is to say not married. That was following Paul's admonition. He said you didn't have to follow him, but, as for himself, he chose to be celibate.

MODERATOR: Okay. In the blue shirt right here.

SPEAKER: In Matthew 1:25 it says that "he kept her a virgin until she gave birth to a son, and she called him named Jesus." The word "until" means something changed.

KEATING: The word "until" in the Greek, as a translation of Hebrew or Aramaic, doesn't have the same force it does in English. It doesn't mean that the event that we might expect necessarily happened afterwards. Similarly with other words. When we say that Jesus was the firstborn, that doesn't mean that there was a second-born of Mary. Under the Mosaic Law, any firstborn child had certain duties and rights. If you had only one child, that child would still be the firstborn. Similarly with the word "until." It doesn't mean that the thing that we might think happened afterwards actually did. It doesn't imply anything about it.

SPEAKER: Okay, in some Scriptures, it's also said that he did not know her "until"—I'd like to refer that back to Genesis where it says that the man knew his wife, which defined the "knew" part.

KEATING: We know what the word "know" means, right? It's a euphemism for marital relations, but again, the key word is "until" in the reference to Joseph and Mary. It doesn't mean that what we might expect actually happened later. It just means it didn't happen up to a certain point.

MODERATOR: Okay. Let's all stand together. We were supposed to have had two 45-minute deliveries and 45 minutes of question. That's two hours and 15 minutes, and it's been four hours.

I appreciate all of you coming. As for these men, they have book tables back there, and I'm going to ask as we're being dismissed for both of them to go back there. You can talk to them, get their literature. I hope it's been beneficial for you to be here tonight.

Thank You!

I hope you found this little book useful or entertaining—preferably both! If you did, please consider leaving an honest review at Amazon. It is through reviews that writers find most of their new readers.

If you have feedback about the book, I'd like to have it. You can write to me at Karl@KarlKeating.com.

The Books in This Series

The Debating Catholicism Series consists of four short books and an omnibus volume. They are:

Book 1: *The Bible Battle* (Karl Keating vs. Peter S. Ruckman)

Book 2: *High Desert Showdown* (Karl Keating vs. Jim Blackburn)

Book 3: *Tracking Down the True Church* (Karl Keating vs. Jose Ventilacion)

Book 4: *Face Off with an Ex-Priest* (Karl Keating vs. Bartholomew F. Brewer)

Omnibus Volume: *Debating Catholicism* (includes all four books above)

Other Books by Karl Keating

Apologetics the English Way

Can a reasonable case be made for Catholicism? Maybe even a compelling case? Or does the Catholic argument falter? Does it wilt before critiques from top-notch opponents? Judge for yourself. You don't have to be Catholic or even religious to relish the intellectual sparring that goes on in these pages.

Here is high-level controversial writing, culled from Karl Keating's favorite books. Each selection is a forceful exposition of Catholic truth. Most are from the 1930s, all come from English Catholics, and all are aimed at a single antagonist, with the public invited to look over the writer's shoulder. The reader can view the weaknesses and occasional mistakes even of his own champion.

These pages are filled with vivid personalities. These were men who knew the Catholic faith and could explain it to others. The individuals against whom they wrote may not have been converted—one or two were, in the long run—but any number of readers of these little-known masterpieces must have found their faith bolstered and their doubts assuaged. The issues covered in these exchanges are still discussed today—but probably nowhere in as glorious a style as here.

The New Geocentrists

Were Copernicus, Galileo, and Kepler wrong? Does Earth orbit the Sun, or does the Sun orbit Earth? For centuries, everyone thought the science was settled, but today the accepted cosmology is being challenged by writers, speakers, and movie producers who insist that science took a wrong turn in the seventeenth century. These new geocentrists claim not only that Earth is the center of our planetary system but that Earth is motionless at the very center of the universe.

They insist they have the science to back up their claims, which they buttress with evidence from the Bible and Church documents. But do they have a case? How solid is their reasoning, and how trustworthy are they as interpreters of science and theology?

The New Geocentrists examines the backgrounds, personalities, and arguments of the people involved in what they believe is a revolutionary movement, one that will overthrow the existing cosmological order and, as a consequence, change everyone's perception of the status of mankind.

No Apology

Karl Keating has been a Catholic apologist for nearly four decades. In these pages he shares some of his own experiences and some stories from times past. He writes about how to do apologetics and how not to. He defends the very idea of apologetics against a theologian who thinks apologetics is passé. He looks at how the faith is promoted through beauty and through suffering. He takes you from his own backyard to such distant times and places as fifth-century Jerusalem and sixteenth-century Japan.

Anti-Catholic Junk Food

You are what you eat. That is as true of the mind as of the body. Eat enough greasy food, and your silhouette will betray your culinary preferences. Give credence to enough greasy ideas, and your mind will be as flabby as your waistline. This book looks at eight examples of religious junk food, things that have come across Karl Keating's desk during his career as a Catholic apologist. You likely will find these morsels unconvincing and unpalatable, as you should. The problem is that plenty of people—including people on your block—consider such stuff to be intellectual high cuisine.

Jeremiah's Lament

For many, the best way to reach an understanding of the Catholic Church is to see how other people misunderstand it. This book is full of misunderstandings.

The people quoted in these pages came to their confusions in various ways. Sometimes it was by reading the wrong books or by failing to read the right books. Sometimes it was a matter of heredity, with prejudices passed down from father to son and from mother to daughter. At other times errors were imbibed at the foot of the pulpit, in the university lecture hall, or from door-to-door missionaries.

Whatever their origin, misunderstandings are misunderstandings. They should be recognized for what they are and set aside, even if that means a break from personal habit or family tradition. More than a century ago, Pope Leo XIII noted that there is nothing so salutary as to understand the world as it really is. That is true particularly of the Church that Christ established because to misunderstand her is to misunderstand him.

How to Fail at Hiking Mt. Whitney

Often, the best way to succeed at something is to learn how to fail at it—and then to avoid the things that lead to failure. There are books that tell you how to succeed at hiking Mt. Whitney. This book helps you *not* to fail by showing you what *not* to do, from the moment you start planning your trip to the moment you reach the summit.

You learn what gear not to buy and not to take, how to maximize your chances of getting a hiking permit (don't apply for the wrong days of the week!), how to prepare yourself physically without over-preparing, how to avoid being laid low by altitude or weather problems, how not to take too much food or water—or too little. You even discover how to shave a mile off the trip by using little-known shortcuts that can make the difference between reaching the summit and reaching exhaustion.

Most people who depart the Mt. Whitney trailhead fail to reach the top. Some fail because of things entirely beyond their control, but many fail because of insufficient preparation, false expectations, and basic errors of judgment. Their mistakes can come at the beginning (such as failing to get a hiking permit), during the preparation stage (such as being induced to buy "bombproof" gear), or during the hike (such as not heeding bodily warning signs).

Through engaging stories of his own and others' failures, Karl Keating shows you how to fail—and therefore how to succeed—at hiking the tallest peak in the 48 contiguous states.

About Karl Keating

Karl Keating holds advanced degrees in theology and law (University of San Diego) plus an honorary doctor of laws degree (Ave Maria University). He founded Catholic Answers, the English-speaking world's largest lay-run Catholic apologetics organization. His best-known books are *Catholicism and Fundamentalism* (nearly a quarter-million paperback copies sold) and *What Catholics Really Believe* (about half that many sold). His avocations include hiking, studying languages, and playing the baroque mandolino. He lives in San Diego. You can follow him at his author website and on Facebook:

KarlKeating.com
Facebook.com/KarlKeatingBooks

www.ingramcontent.com/pod-product-compliance
Lightning Source LLC
Chambersburg PA
CBHW060708030426
42337CB00017B/2801

* 9 7 8 1 9 4 2 5 9 6 1 9 6 *